AFRICAN WRITERS SERIES

Editorial Adviser · Chinua Achebe

15

Origin East Africa

AFRICAN WRITERS SERIES

Origin East Africa

A MAKERERE ANTHOLOGY

devised and edited by
DAVID COOK

HEINEMANN
LONDON IBADAN NAIROBI

Heinemann Educational Books Ltd
48 Charles Street, London W1X 8AH
PBM 5205, Ibadan · POB 25080, Nairobi
MELBOURNE TORONTO AUCKLAND
HONG KONG SINGAPORE

SBN 435 90015 3
© Heinemann Educational Books Ltd 1965
Introduction © David Cook 1965

First published 1965
Reprinted 1966, 1969

Printed in Malta by
St Paul's Press Ltd

Contents

CONTENTS

Titles of poems are in italics

Joe Mutiga's poem, *To the Ceremonial Mugumo,* first appeared in *Transition 3,* and we are grateful to the editor for permission to reproduce this.

Introduction

When I first started looking around to see what Makerere students had written in the past, and what they are capable of writing now, I had no thoughts of making an anthology. I wanted to read whatever there was to be read as a process of private discovery. And further to this, I was trying to resolve certain questions that were running through my mind.

I had become convinced that many students who seek to study English at Makerere (perhaps the same thing is true of all African university colleges) do so because they themselves want to write. My own experience as student and lecturer in British universities had made me realize that the traditional pattern of advanced English studies tends more to discourage young authors than to draw them out. The practice of literary criticism should not only sharpen all one's sensibilities, but should also offer a positive challenge to everyone with creative urges. In practice, in raising a student's standards and his awareness, the study of literature all too often fills him with disgust at his own fumblings with words, and therefore inhibits him from thinking of himself as a potential author. I wanted to find out how an English course could best link criticism and creativity.

Naturally the first thing to do was to look at student writing, past and present. The chief sources at Makerere were *Penpoint*, the English Department magazine, started in 1958, and original course work undertaken as part of the study of style. I was surprised and delighted with what I found. Soon I thought that some of the forgotten material was worth resurrecting; and some of the current work worth carpentering. I discussed the whole matter with James Ngugi, then a second year student, and we began sifting – a long process, in the course of which other members of the department were encouraging and helpful. At length we had a varied but unwieldy miscellany. Only when we had whittled this down to half did we come to the conclusion that what remained deserved formal publication.

Once the volume had been accepted, serious editorial work began. The collection draws on seventeen issues of *Penpoint*, the sixteenth, which came out while I was at work on the volume, being the first to be professionally printed. The material reflects two vital qualities of Makerere: its cosmopolitan nature, but also its essential East Africanness. Twenty of the twenty-five contributors are from homes scattered all over Kenya, the Republic of Tanzania and Uganda; while the remainder comprise a Nigerian, two Malawians, an American and a Briton. Every writer has been urged to improve upon the original version of his work, without changing its intrinsic nature or form. Many suggestions were made, which the authors accepted, bettered or rejected with complete freedom. Most of the writers reacted to comments independently and vigorously.

I think only one item remains exactly as it first appeared in *Penpoint*, down to the very last comma. At the other extreme David Rubadiri, whose three poems have already figured in other anthologies, has here completely recast them, reflecting his startling development as a poet. Only two other contributions have previously been included in books (as far as I know), Gatuiria's poem '*Kariuki*' and James Ngugi's story '*The Fig Tree*' (now considerably revised); though three stories have figured in periodicals subsequent to their original appearance in *Penpoint*.

The selection was made simply on the merit of each item, except that no room could be found for any critical or discursive articles. I would roughly divide the writings in the book into two groups, without bothering to ask myself exactly where the dividing line falls. The first group embraces work which I find to be of a very high quality on an absolute standard and which anyone anywhere who is interested in good writing in English should be glad to read; I think some of these authors will in time establish themselves. Secondly, the book includes work which I think deserves the attention of anyone more especially interested in the development of writing in Africa. Just as enthusiasts for, say, eighteenth-century literature, or space fiction, will welcome some writings which would not concern the general reader, so those of us who find African writing specially interesting and significant will be pleased to read stories which we might not press upon outsiders. However, with some help from James Ngugi, I have intended to exclude whatever is simply mediocre.

I have been much impressed with the seriousness and hard work that has gone into these writings, even those which the authors had not originally thought to show to anyone. These are not chance hits by lucky beginners. Challenge a detail in one of these poems, and you will find the poet can tell you how he came to put that particular word there, and the struggle he had to find it. East African restraint and economy of wording may surprise some readers; while the deliberate, forceful rejection of melodrama in the unwinding of many of the stories may be misinterpreted by those who look for the 'well-made' dramatic dénouement so common in European tradition.

This is not a critical edition. I believe that original work presented for the first time should not be coloured in any way by an editor's personal views further than is inevitable in the process of selection. Schoolboys and girls must have the same chance as adults to assess for themselves the writing that is going on around them. Later, if a writer becomes established, any critical views will fall into perspective.

I am asked what I hope this anthology will achieve. The main answer is that it aims to make available a volume of writing which is worth reading in its own right. I hope also that it will encourage some of the authors represented to write more; I would like to help overcome the exaggerated diffidence and modesty that holds back so many young African authors (the reasons for which are not far to seek). In schools I hope the book will provide both a body of material which is by its nature intensely interesting, and by its influence will help to make children here feel that all literature really belongs to them, rather than simply coming from the outside, to be shared on sufferance; and that it will spur and encourage African boys and girls to write confidently, vigorously and independently themselves.

Finally, a brief word about the fact that this book is all in English. Writers are men who respect language, in the way a painter respects paint. It makes no sense, I believe, to respect one language more than another. All languages have an authority similar in kind. I cannot feel that they are in competition in Africa. English is not a mother tongue in East Africa; nor, however, is it foreign – it has let down its own roots here; technically speaking it is a 'second language'. What a positive power Africans enjoy is thus *possessing* two fundamentally different languages! If the Russians and Americans and Chinese could *really* understand each other's words, could bridge that gulf in communication, what a different world this would be – how many barriers to human community would dissolve! Sometimes Africans choose to write in Swahili or Yoruba, Luganda or Kikuyu. At other times they choose to write in East African English or Ghanaian English or other forms of English (as some authors write in West Indian and American and Welsh English). This is a volume of writings in English by past and present Makerere students.

Makerere   DAVID COOK
July 1964

Violet Kokunda

KEFA KAZANA

As I stepped out of the house, I stood on the threshold for a minute blinded by the sharp, direct rays of the sun. It was a very hot afternoon and I thought that really luck had dealt unfairly with me by making my turn fall on such a day. Mama was still enjoying her siesta and my sisters were somewhere no doubt making the best of their freedom. It was my turn to prepare afternoon tea.

I filled the kettle and as I was about to enter the kitchen I thought I saw something creep backwards behind the wall. Yes, there was a small boy in rags. I called out to him, 'What are you hiding out there for, boy? Come here and let's have a look at you.'

He looked terrified of me. Had I said something unkind? So I hastily added, 'What's your name, boy?'

'Kefa . . . Kefa Kazana,' he added.

'Kefa,' I repeated absently. I remembered the kettle I was holding and I hurried to the kitchen, picking up some logs for lighting the fire as I went.

'Well, Kefa Kazara, you'd better come in here and help with this cooking,' I called back.

He came slowly and sat humbly on the edge of the doorstep.

'Where do you come from, Kefa Kazara?'

'Kefa Kazana,' he corrected me timidly.

'Yes, Kazana, where is your home?'

'I have no home.' His voice was hardly audible.

'No home! Nonsense. Of course you have a home; everybody has a home where his daddy, mummy, sisters and brothers live. Where do your parents live?'

'I don't have no parents. They are . . . They were . . .' I saw that the subject was making him terribly miserable so I cut in quickly: 'Never mind that now. . . .' And the kettle was boiling. 'Well, stay here for a minute, Kazana, while I go and prepare tea,' and as he looked longingly at the kettle I assured him that I would call him when everything was ready. And it suddenly struck me as I looked over his bare, meagre body that he might be starving and had come to beg for food. And how his rags smelt. Lord!

The sun had gone down a little and I thought it would be lovely to have our tea outside. I brought mats and spread them under the tree and, when everything was nice and ready, I went to the house.

'Tea is ready, Mama – and there is a small, awful-looking boy who is very hungry. He says he has no home, no daddy, and no mummy.'

'Well, thank God you still have yours, and show your gratitude by being more respectful. Don't stand like that in the doorway while I'm dressing,' she stormed at me. Really – I wondered whether Kefa Kazana was not better off after all.

I ran back to the kitchen and as I came near I heard something crash on the floor. Kazana started and then faced me a little fearfully. He had been scraping the remains of our last meal out of the dish. I pretended not to have noticed anything and I told him to wash his hands and come to tea.

'I don't think that I'd better really,' he said timorously.

'Why not?' I asked, tracing his glance to the far corner of the house where my three robust sisters had emerged.

'Oh, don't mind those, they are just my sisters.'

'But they are so many and they might beat me like the others.'

'Come on, they will not beat you; they dare not; I am their big sister, you see.'

'But those others beat me. They beat me because I ate their dog's food.'

'You ate their dog's food?'

'They didn't want it and I was very hungry. They said I was too dirty.'

'Well, that may be, but my sisters won't beat you. You will see.'

He came and sat about ten yards away from us. All eyes were turned on him and I hastened to explain that he was Kefa Kazana and had no home, no daddy, no mummy.

'Which cup will he drink out of?' whispered Norah.

'I should say Juliet's,' returned Mary, glancing at his rags. Juliet was our cat.

'Juliet's, a cat's dish!' exclaimed Mother, without bothering to lower her voice. 'Run and bring one of the visitors' cups, Norah.'

'The visitors' cups!' I joined in the chorus. At that very moment Emmanuel appeared. We had all forgotten about him.

'Whence cometh this ragamuffin? Out of my sight before I am tempted to throw a stone at you. I want to have my tea,' said he, humorously he thought.

We all turned on him in anger but before we could say a word, Kefa Kazana had jumped up, and had shot towards the thick elephant grass behind the kitchen. My little sisters ran after him calling him to come back and have his tea first. Our shouts of 'Kefa Kazana' echoed through the dry banana garden, over the empty fields and down into the valley below.

'And he has no home, no daddy, no mummy,' repeated somebody as our shouts spontaneously ceased.

Joseph Waiguru

THE ROUND MUD HUT

The round warm hut
Proud to the last
Of her noble sons
And daughters
Stands besieged.

Of late, stones,
In tripartite agreement,
Guarded a fire.
And then a pot,
A large hot pot
Which nurtured
Black, black children.

Near the door
Stands a thin-necked pot,
Guard to the entrance,
Hiding cold, cold water,
Water cold
As the morning dew.

Three thick gourds
Firm on the floor
Near the wall
Have in them something,

Something sour-sweet,
Which, three days past,
Was tasteless.

That is a mat tray,
The work of a skilled hand;
Abundant with food,
Yes, ten round lumps,
It's generous to all.

There's a shelf,
Masterpiece to a carpenter
Specialized in wood and string,
On it rests
Calabashes large and small.
Their sum who knows?

See five stools,
Three three-legged,
Two four-legged,
Worn smooth through use.

Up there,
A high, high shelf,
Higher than man standing,
Covered with soot,
A story strange it tells;
Fires have burnt, and burnt.

And there's a bed,
No, more than one:
Many goats have died
To make the bedspread.

The bleating sheep
And the horned goat,
Calves cud-chewing

At that end penned,
Share the warmth
Of the round mud hut.

All this and much more,
Slowly and slowly disappears:
Slowly and slowly iron appears,
Lays a siege on the roof
And takes prisoner the pot and the gourd.
The plate, the cup, the lamp,
What's this but a change
To the new oblong house?
The round mud hut is no more.

THE BEACH

The cold grey sea and the warm blue sky,
High majestic waves on this sandy shore break,
And the water waltzing recedes:
Yet little streams, streams tiny left,
Swiftly twist their way amid tiny rocks.
The crushing music and the dance,
Over and over again, night and day,
Day and night repeated. The step, the motion,
All the same, today and tomorrow the same.
The rising sun, that orange ball behind misty air,
Only the early bird that with the sun rises
Welcomes the charm, the beauty of the first ray.
Rolling along that blue wall high above,
The sun chases the cowardly mist away.
But for the hiss and the din of dying bubbles
I'd call this yet another day up home:
Here comes a couple whose faces tell experience.
And there a pair whose walk spells youth.

And who is that but a family of four?
What pleasure do they seek on this shore,
No, from this water, this sand, this coast?
See how soon this place teems with life!
Man: all colours and all shades; all, all here.

THE UNTILLED FIELD

Mwangi thought of nobody else but his wife Wanjiku. She was
lazy; always going to work late in the day when everybody else
had already done half their digging. By the time she reached the
field, it was already so hot that to lift a hoe was almost a torture.
The heat of the sun disturbed the flies from their rest so that they
buzzed around her as she slowly lifted her tool. She had to drop
it again to strike the biting fly. There was no point in continuing
to labour. After all she would come here tomorrow and the day
after. Even the day after that she would be here. She sat down in
the cool shade of a *muthaithi* tree and soon fell asleep. Mwangi
watched her from afar, where he was herding his cattle. By now
it was his field alone which lay untilled, and the rains were near.
An hour went by, two hours, three hours and Wanjiku still slept.
Was she dead? Could a snake have bitten her? He would have
heard cries. Mwangi decided to find out.

He left his cattle and slowly approached the spot where his
wife lay. He looked back to see whether the cattle would stray far
before he returned to them. Satisfied that they would not, he
moved on. He quickened his step, hoping that she would wake
up before he reached her. He did not want to show her that he
had all along been watching her. But he would never be satisfied
until he knew whether or not his wife's expression betrayed any
guilty conscience for the neglect of her duties. He changed his
pace. Quietly he stalked her as a lion stealthily hunts a deer, or
like a cobra just about to strike. He feared to make a rustle.
Mwangi remembered the cows and goats he had paid her father as

a dowry. The marriage feast surpassed any he had ever seen, or even heard of. Is this the wife he had married, the woman he had so dearly paid for? Was she created only for child-bearing? What was she for? He would soon learn from the appearance of her face when asleep. He reached her. There she was, sleeping like a log, except that a log does not breathe. The sight shocked him. Where he had expected to find at least a slight element of guilt, he found only a pure, peaceful, calm face – only blissful happiness. Wanjiku was content to lie idle, a basket, a hoe and a *panga* by her side. He stood there, not knowing what to do next. His mind was as blank as a white sheet. At last, his lips set as if to smile and then changed into a grin which looked sinister. His jaw dropped, showing milky-white teeth. He thought of beating her with the thick walking-stick he was carrying and then that evening sending her packing to her father's. No, he would gain nothing by such an action. After all, women were just little, defenceless creatures. He was annoyed when he realized he could not beat her. Oh, but she was beautiful too! He knelt down and touched her lips with the back of his right hand, moving the fingers along them. She stirred and turned face downwards, but did not open her eyes. Mwangi was furious with himself and with her. He turned to see what work she had done – there was no sign of freshly dug ground. She should have finished this field since she informed him that she had started on it, but at this rate she would not have completed even half of it before the rains poured madly down. Would she ever wake? After deciding not to disturb her, he quickly went back to his cattle.

Mwangi thought for a moment. Then he rounded up his animals and drove them home at the greatest speed the beasts could manage. He shut them in a shed, though it was only two o'clock, and hurriedly took out a hoe from his hut. There was no time to lose, and within fifteen minutes he was back in the field. Wanjiku was still sleeping. He would not wake her up: that he had resolved the moment he decided to take his cattle home.

Mwangi planted his feet firmly on the ground and lifted the hoe high over his head. He struck the first blow on the too, too soft earth. He struck another and yet another. Thud, thud, thud

went the hoe, on and on. He laboured and was never tired.
Drops of sweat flowed down his face and their sour taste only
added more energy to his stout arms. Lumps of earth were
following him as he proceeded farther and farther away from
where he had started. He neither looked back nor forwards, lest
the length of the field he had to dig should discourage him. All
he saw was the place where he had to push in his hoe. He laboured
on. He was twenty yards away when Wanjiku woke up and saw
him. What was it? She looked up at the sun in the sky and knew
it was half past three; the time she started collecting firewood.
Was she always sleeping like this? She watched mesmerized as
he dug and dug.

Mwangi stopped for breath without looking back. The sweat
was too much. His shirt and trousers were glued to his body. He
dropped the hoe, took off his clothes and then cut a banana leaf
which he tied round his waist. He then picked up the hoe, lifted it
and once again resumed his work. As Wanjiku watched, he
moved farther and farther away from her. He furiously attacked
the ground which was becoming as stubborn as a mule. His black
frame dripped wet and as drops of sweat flowed down his whole
body, they cut lines in the red dust which had stuck to his skin.
The more he turned the ground, the madder he grew.

Suddenly, Wanjiku stood up and picked up her hoe. She
rushed to his side and wanted to stop him. He barked at her and
she gave up. Within a few minutes, he was ahead of her by six
feet. He would not rest until the work was over. Was he her
husband any more? Certainly. With a force she had never felt
before, she went to his right-hand side and started digging. She
would dig as long as he dug, and stop when he stopped. If they
were to die, they would die together. She soon caught up and
fell into step with him. The earth was softer than she had ever
known it to be. They dug and never stopped to see what work
they had done. Neither was thinking of the other but only of
their field. The sun was, however, faster than they were and the
last flickers of light would soon disappear. They went on and on,
and neither dared to speak. It was cool now, and a soft breeze
blew over them but was not enough to dry away the sweat. In

unison, they attacked the enemy who had brought them together. It grew dark but they never thought of going home. They saw the edge of the field and stopped petrified. Only two feet away! They looked at one another and then at the edge. They turned back and could not see where they had started. With smiles they embraced and fell down. There they lay till the following morning when they woke up as if from a dream, completely satisfied of their future life together.

M. M. Haji

WHEN THE WALLS CAME TUMBLING DOWN

Kassim felt he was the only one of the family who was not shocked. Of course his brother, Hemed, didn't count. He couldn't think of anything that could shock him.

'Get over it quick. Someone else will come along soon.' He reminded him of the gentleman who said that women were like buses: it was not worth-while running for them; another one would come along if you waited a bit more.

Kassim smiled. As if you could always wait! Couldn't you, though? You waited for eight o'clock to go to the office; you read the papers while waiting for lunch or supper or a bus: you lived as you waited to die! Perhaps one could do both. Wait and live together.

But then Esha was like that. One could never know what she would do next; she would do most unexpected things, but somehow quite expected – of her. Two weeks ago when they were engaged she was quite definite: she didn't love Ibrahim, her cousin, any more.

And this morning she married Ibrahim and looked wonderfully happy. There wasn't anything he could do about it, was there?

Once he tried to persuade Esha that life was infinitely rich. Hemed agreed, with reservations of course: 'But not *your* life: like your art, that is one-sided.' Kassim did not understand this. Every life must have limitations. But its limitations should be part of its richness. And yet could he be sure what he himself meant by that?

He slowed down to negotiate a steep turning. Now the setting sun was behind him. The road in front of him was fringed with palm-trees and thick bushes full of wild flowers. They were orange with the last rays of the sun. He saw himself driving into the golden light.

Near the top of the hill he stopped the car. He looked down at the wide valley, as he had done dozens of times. He saw the rice plantations, flushed, stretching away below him. The little stream meandered its marshy course and lost itself out of sight. There was more of it farther down but one didn't see it. He had only a vague picture of it in his mind like something that happened long ago and which one couldn't quite forget.

He felt the enveloping peace flow into him. He looked; and the feeling of being lost in a maze of mystery was creeping into him. He could let himself be lost, for, like the stream, he would later find himself. But what if only to be lost again? Like the stream: to be lost into the Deep. And he was afraid with the fear of things that pushed themselves up to be remembered.

Dusk was falling fast. He thought he was relieved, but then there would be the darkness of the night. And things looked so strange in the dark. And then when morning came they would still persist in retaining their strange forms in spite of the light. Could it be only false light or was it the forms that were false? It was difficult for one who couldn't believe that both were real.

But Kassim had not yet learnt to think so far. It was now quite dark. On the other side, beyond the hills, the horizon was losing colour. It was growing pale, he thought, like a face in fear. Once he overheard Hemed telling Esha that Kassim was afraid of fear. Hemed was only being foolish again and talking in riddles, as he always did. Not that anyone understood him, least of all Esha. She only said she didn't know, she loved him and that was all. She was happy. Evidently she didn't love him now. Perhaps not even then. And that was that. He no longer imagined that people could be happy, because they didn't understand; because they did not want to understand; and preferred to live in the dark that was the darkness of Death rather than die to live otherwise. Yet perhaps it was possible people really did not know they were missing anything.

Kassim wanted to start the car, but the night fascinated him; strangely, he thought. Hemed once told him that his art and their mother were things he took refuge in. Took refuge from what? Really Hemed was the limit!

He started the car and switched on the headlights. He drove through the lighted path that continued up the hill. The darkness that bounded it merged immediately behind him. Only he did not turn to look.

Below, the road took a sharp turn; and before he could apply the brakes, a wild dog bounded in front of him. There was a sharp yelp and then only the sound of the engine. He stopped. He knew the dog was lying there, but he wouldn't get down. A strange fear was seizing him by the throat and he felt as if he was being choked. He looked helplessly around. There was only darkness there. After a long minute of agonizing indecision, he opened the door and got down.

The dog was clearly dying. It was seized in convulsions and a savage fear was in its eyes. Again Kassim looked around. Darkness. He looked back at the dog and the savage eyes held him. They held him until he no longer saw them.

Instead, he saw something else. Ten years dissolved away and he saw himself on the beach . . .

Kassim was angry. Salma wouldn't come out of the water and he knew he couldn't go home and leave her there. It was his own idea that the two of them had gone down to swim. And Mother had permitted them to go only after he had promised to look after his little sister. He lay flat on the smooth white sand and began to draw the palm-trees before him. Afterwards he turned. And Salma was no longer there.

He was on the beach the next morning when they brought up her body. He ran down madly, hoping – childishly, but hoping. Then he saw it. The body. He froze. He didn't utter a single cry. He never cried, never wept – even afterwards . . .

Now his body shook; sobs that choked him were audible

above the sound of the running engine of his car. They sounded fierce: as would be the fire that could be kindled from cold dead ashes. And tears ran down his face as if they had been collecting there in a kind of reservoir for ten years. It seemed hours. And all the time he was also seeing the face of Esha. Her puzzled face; her hurt face; and her happy face.

He calmed down. He wiped his eyes and saw the dog that was lying there – still; dead. His face was sad. But it was no longer the face of fear. Sad and exhausted.

Kassim went into the living-room. His mother looked up from her knitting. 'And what have you been doing all this time?' she asked.

'I was thinking of coming to look for you. We thought you had had an accident,' Hemed said.

'Well, I had, in a way. I ran over a wild dog and it died.'

His mother looked at him anxiously. Hemed said, 'I'll go out and bury it in the morning.'

'No need. I have already done so.'

Hemed looked at him incredulously and then nodded his head slowly several times, frowning severely.

'There is a letter for you,' his mother said; 'I think it is from Esha.' Kassim took the letter from his mother, opened it and began to read quietly.

'Well?' his mother inquired.

'She says she is sorry, and could I ever forgive her?' There was silence.

Kassim noticed that his brother still had a faraway look on his face, without the frown. He himself looked like a man who, after having uprooted a long thought from out of the depth of years, watched it merge with ordinary things; without exhaustion; as of a volcano after having thrown out hot and melted rocks, as the earth shook and trembled; still: long before the mind had ceased to labour one knew that one was reborn. For a wise man died many times before his death.

'She was too hasty, unfortunately.' Hemed broke the long silence. 'If she had only not married him today . . .'

Kassim looked at him – as before – suspecting mockery of his own thoughts. But there was none. And Kassim looked as he did after spending long hours mixing his colours, obtaining an exact shade.

He nodded his head, like a man coming out of sleep, and saw that dawn was really come; and that in a full day there was light and darkness . . .

. . . And that man had to learn to live in both.

NOTHING EXTRAORDINARY

After a stay of one week, Esha had gone back to town and to Ibrahim. Phone calls had come in a succession which later had become almost exasperating. There had not, however, been any indication that Ibrahim had grown suspicious. Even she herself had not thought that things would turn out as they had done.

It was not so with Hemed. He had watched helplessly as his worst fears materialized under his nose. Mrs Rauf had suspected that something was in the air, but refrained from making any comment since she had not been exactly sure of the position, and no one had seen fit to enlighten her. Mr Rauf had gone in his usual easy-going, humorous way without the faintest idea what had been hatching under his own roof.

Now he was delighted to learn that his son was writing an article on indigenous art. He had no idea what that meant, of course. But it sounded progressive and superior. And he was pleased. Though Kassim was not the type of person after his own heart, he was proud of him.

At the announcement the previous night that Kassim would be going to town and staying in their house there in order to be near the library, Hemed had looked up at his brother with troubled eyes. But Kassim had deliberately refused to meet his gaze and had walked away directly to his own room.

Now all the family came out to see Kassim off in his car. He said good-bye without looking at his elder brother though he felt his painful gaze on him. He switched on the engine and in a moment drove away under the forenoon sun.

Kassim rose from his desk and went to his bedroom. He lay on his bed and lit a cigarette. He glanced at the clock on the top of the radio. It was just after ten in the morning. He had been here two days but Esha had neither called nor communicated in any way. She was perhaps being wise, but Kassim was finding the waiting rather strenuous.

He frowned, and for a moment forgot the cigarette between his fingers. . . .

Esha had a right to her own life, hadn't she? Kassim almost smiled. What nonsense had been spoken about rights! A right to one's life. One was tempted to agree that rights were only creatures of the imagination: the imagination of someone who finds himself in a situation such as his own at present; the imagination of the weak who discover no other way of holding on to what they possess or think they possess; or of pursuing their own desires. Perhaps life itself was indeed a continuous struggle in pursuit of one desire after another. And rights were nothing more than one of the tricks of the trade. Only one had to be very brave to believe in such things. Or perhaps very cowardly.

He heard the outside door open and shut. And before he had time to hope or fear that it was Esha, she stood in his bedroom doorway, veiled. He jumped up from the bed and stood in the middle of the room, lost. He certainly did not take her in his arms as he had planned half a dozen times. Esha stepped in coolly, and he followed her gaze round the small room. He realized now that it was in a queer state. The bed needed tidying; there was no chair in the room; a small occasional table carried his portable radio and the clock; opposite the bed an old carpet covered about half the floor; it was littered with piles of books; and old newspapers and periodicals were scattered everywhere; his clothes hung from nails on the wall near the door; apart from the chest of drawers whose top was covered with brushes, combs, boot polish, used envelopes and writing material, there was nothing else in the room in the way of furniture.

Murmuring a faint apology, Kassim hurried out of the room to get a chair. Esha was getting out of her veil when he returned. He placed the chair at the edge of the carpet, facing the bed, and with a weak gesture of his arm offered it to her. She folded her veil slowly without looking at him, and then placed it on the back on the chair. She sat down and crossed her legs. Kassim stood in front of her, again lost. She had arrived too soon.

He turned and started to tidy up the bed. Realizing what he was doing he grew embarrassed and stopped, feeling hot at the back of his neck. He turned again to face Esha with apologetic eyes. But Esha was smiling. He smiled back. Soon they were laughing.

Esha stood up and began to move about the room putting things in place. Kassim sat on the chair she had vacated and followed her every movement, fascinated. She was not more than twenty-two, four years his junior, slim of figure and fair. Her small nose was, thought Kassim, the most fascinating feature of her face.

Two hours later she broke his world of rapture.

'I think I should go now,' she said. 'Ibrahim will be getting back from the office soon.'

Ibrahim. He had almost forgotten about Ibrahim. He reached for his cigarettes and lit one. He inhaled deeply and then slowly let the smoke escape from his mouth. He watched the smoke as it passed easily through the mosquito-net. As things would pass by those who did not understand, who would not perceive a lighted match nor the small glow of fire. The fire would in time be put out, or would die by itself. Yes. The little spark of fire would in time die away without starting a conflagration. Kassim frowned, seeing he had to decide again, or suffer further the punishment of uncertainty.

Esha got down from the bed and began to put on her veil. Perhaps what she showed him of her heart was beautifully veiled. To deceive them both.

'I told the houseboy I was going out shopping,' he heard her saying.

He nodded his head in answer to her good-bye. And continued

to lie there on his bed, still frowning. But when at length he rose, the expression on his face was defiant.

Indigenous Art was getting on satisfactorily. Esha came almost every day during the following week.

Kassim rose from his desk and went back to his bedroom to get dressed. It was about seven in the evening. He had met Ibrahim the previous night. He had blamed him for not calling and had invited him to dinner that night.

He found himself making an effort to laugh at Ibrahim's countless jokes. Esha as usual looked cool and composed.

At length Kassim managed to inquire how Ibrahim was getting on with his job. He was employed in a firm which sold motor spares and did a little in the way of repairs.

'Fine,' he replied and fell silent

'He doesn't like the manager,' Esha added.

Kassim said, 'Oh,' and another silence followed. But that was only because Ibrahim was thinking of the manager, and wondering why some people were so queer. Kassim continued to look down at his plate, hunched. Like a man carrying a heavy burden, he felt its weight grown two-fold.

Shortly Ibrahim's face lit up again.

'I shall be going away on a business trip for the week-end,' he said, like a child announcing a holiday to the Mediterranean.

Kassim's heart missed a beat. He waited almost breathlessly.

'I was thinking that Esha would feel rather lonely,' he continued. 'Then I remembered that you are here.' He smiled at Kassim innocently. Kassim murmured, 'Yes,' without raising his eyes from his plate. Esha got up to fetch more drinks. Kassim looked up at her, and almost hated her for it.

They were lying side by side on their towels. Behind them the sun was setting. The palm-trees threw tall slender shadows across the brown sandy beach. Their heads were lost among the gently whispering waves as if, Kassim thought, hiding in dread of their imminent extinction. Several fishing boats had been beached and were lying piteously on their sides, as if prostrating themselves before the land. Kassim shifted his gaze quickly across the bay and watched a group of low-lying islands almost enclosing it, like a giant bowl of some strange deeply orange wine. And the feeling returned that there was a silent music in beauty. One could let oneself be borne aloft on its invisible wings to the farthest confines of the spheres. And there be lost in No-Time. Kassim felt himself delighted with the delight of a mystery that was no longer fearsome, though still inexplicable.

He got up on one elbow and looked at the childishly happy face of Esha. He bent his head to kiss her smooth neck. She closed her eyes, and then reached out with her hands to pull him closer towards her.

And as light faded away, dusk gathered its strength to surrender itself, with them, to darkness.

Sunday afternoon.

Esha crossed the street and entered a large general store. She lowered her veil as she saw a young lady of her own age hurrying towards her, hugging a large basket of stores on her high bosom with one hand, while frantically trying to keep her veil in place with the other.

'Well, well . . . if it isn't Esha,' she cried.

'Zenab! what are you doing in town? I thought you were in the country. How is Salim?'

'He is all right. I hope so. I haven't seen him for ages.'

Esha looked puzzled.

'One gets tired of the country,' Zenab continued, 'and husbands can be such bores.'

'Well, I— Where are you staying?'

At that moment a muscular young man advanced and relieved Zenab of the basket. He smiled sheepishly at the two of them and marched away towards the counter. Zenab smiled.

'He is a dear,' she remarked.

Esha, still uncertain, asked, 'Who is he?'

'Oh, just a friend.' Esha did not fail to notice the mischievous twinkle in her eyes.

'Oh, don't look so shocked. These things happen, dear. It's

nothing extraordinary,' she smiled again, and the twinkle returned.

'How is Ibrahim?'

'He is all right. At this moment he is away . . .'

'You must be enjoying yourself,' Zenab cut in. This time she definitely winked at her. And before Esha could think how to reply, she said good-bye, hurried to the counter and swept the young giant away towards the door, turning for a last wave before she disappeared into the street.

Esha stood alone, dazed. She came to, and walked directly to the door and out into the street. A few blocks up the road she turned into a lane. She increased her pace.

And back home she walked straight to her room. An envelope addressed to her lay on her dressing-table. She saw it was in Kassim's handwriting, and she hesitated for a moment before picking it up and opening it. She gasped as she read the note, evidently scrawled in haste. She hurried out of the house again.

Kassim and Hemed, occupying the only two chairs in the room, were silent. The door opened and Esha was ushered in. They rose. Hardly noticing them, her gaze was fixed on the bed. Ibrahim, with a thickly bandaged head and one arm in plaster, opened his heavy, weary eyes to look at his wife.

Esha stood with leaden legs, breathless, and continued to stare. Ibrahim made a weak movement with his other arm. Esha almost ran to the bed, clasped the arm in both her hands, blinded by the flood of tears that was streaming down her face.

Hemed signalled his brother and the two of them left the room on tiptoe.

They went into the waiting-room; and Kassim walked to the open window and looked out through the gathering dusk at the neat garden below. Hemed joined him, and Kassim braced himself as if expecting some kind of an attack. But Hemed only stood there for a moment wrapped in his own thoughts. . . .

Poor Ibrahim. It was like him. A driver entering the main road from a side road was supposed to halt. This one didn't. Ibrahim had expected him to, of course. Yes; Ibrahim always assumed that people would do what was expected of them. . . .

He turned to look at Kassim. And Kassim, sensing his eyes on him, shrank. For he still feared his gaze. With the fear of shame.

After a long moment, they both heard a door open and close softly in the corridor. The two brothers turned, and their eyes met. At that instant Hemed saw into his brother's heart; and his own soared in relief.

Kassim dropped Hemed at their house and drove Esha home. She sat rigidly beside him staring in front of her with unseeing eyes.

'The doctor says he'll be all right,' Kassim broke the long silence.

'Yes,' she answered faintly.

They stopped in front of Ibrahim's house, and Esha roused herself. She opened her handbag and took out a key. She handed this to Kassim. Kassim took it, and after a short pause, said simply:

'It is better so.'

'Yes,' she answered. She opened the door, got out and walked towards the house. She did not turn to look back. The door closed quietly behind her.

Kassim sat there in his car and looked at the key in his hand for a long moment. At length he put it in his pocket and took out a packet of cigarettes. He lit one, placed it in his mouth and switched on his car.

And he drove away into the cool night.

John Nagenda

GAHINI LAKE

I stood at one end of Gahini Lake
Years ago, one evening late,
And saw it stretch away beneath me
With red touches of the dying sun.
Here and there a ripple disturbed the surface
Where a guesting, jesting bird,
Low-flying over the serene quiet water,
Had landed and gone on again.
Beneath me, the silent lake;
Around me, the darkening gloom
Through which, occasionally, a bush stood out
In courageous, defiant loneliness.
And there might have been one song or two
From an invisible lonely bird.
As I watched, the light was swallowed up
By a darkness rising from the lake;
And points of light across the darkness
Appeared one by one by one.
Beneath me the lake was black
But gurgled and whispered and snored . . .
What was it I had forever lost
In that deserted instant of time?

WHEN THERE IS A HUSH ACROSS THE SKY

When there is a hush across the sky,
And a small cold breeze among the trees,
And a wisp of song like smoke,
And a lone silent leaf
Like a thought
Loosens hold,
Turns over and falls,
You become for me an evermore,
My dearly-mourned.

AND THIS, AT LAST

The young reporter was really very young, and this would be his
first job of note. Indeed the editor had chosen him precisely
because of this. He wanted a picture of innocence to confront the
gouty, irate old boy with. Through the years the old man had
refused to give interviews altogether, or gave them only to
laugh at the newspapermen. Perhaps, somehow, the young man
might appear so innocent that the other would take pity on him,
decide that he was not worth laughing at. There was no harm in
trying, anyway.

And so here he was, bright and eager-looking, but horribly
scared inside, willing himself to knock. In his hand he held a
blue notebook, and tucked away in his shirt pocket was a blue
Biro. But even before he knocked, just as he had convinced
himself that he was going to knock, the door opened and he
found himself face to face with his quarry. At this irreverent
thought, he smiled in spite of himself, but then broke off
abruptly as he found the other's eyes looking down at him,

dispassionately and penetratingly. Immediately he was disconcerted and confused.

'Ah youth, youth,' said the other. 'The time when we can still blush and cry into our coffee! Come in.'

The house had obviously been built for comfort. Cosy old straw chairs, a mellow-looking walking-stick in the corner, two sleepy spears on which the years had settled so that now they looked disused, a gourd, which had gone black with time, hanging against a wall. It was a house full of old memories, of voices now forever silent and faces gone still and empty. The young newspaperman felt almost as if he knew the people who had passed through this house.

And the silence was absolute, so that to look through the window and watch the sunlight racing over the ground until it touched the far hills, and to see, far away, the noiseless movement of a car only seen to be moving by the dust following, and to remember that only two hours ago he had been standing before his editor (a noisy one, that one!), all this seemed impossible.

'Sit down, sit down,' the old man said, almost as if he grudged the younger the privilege of seeing all this for the first time. 'Let me see, you want an interview. Do you understand, young man, that you are the first news-hound I've allowed in here since since . . . Oh! my God, since when? It must have been after the wedding of my eldest grand-daughter, fifteen years ago. But you fellows keep on hounding a man, hounding a man . . .'

He was silent and the young newspaperman could not decide whether he was remembering the wedding, or what, and himself kept quiet, so that the silence settled again and the very house seemed to doze.

'And so he is dead,' the old man said, and the boy knew that somehow the man had left the other memories behind and was talking about the interview. 'That's what you want to ask me about, isn't it? Well listen, boy, you are lucky, because somehow you reminded me of another young man of your age, only he was your age sixty years ago and more. I like you, boy, otherwise I might never have opened my mouth to the papers again. And now he is dead. It becomes increasingly lonely and cold the longer you stay. All your friends gone. On your own. Your wife gone and your children gone. Your grandchildren too full of life to be bothered.'

The old man had a disconcerting habit of hopping from one thing to another without notice and then hopping back again. But somehow his vision was so powerful that he carried the boy with him and together they moved into the past, the one realistically, the other with his imagination. A small bird came and alighted on the window and inquisitively nodded its head up and down, eavesdropping, and then perhaps felt something in the air and with a reproving twitter flew off for merrier pastimes.

'He and I grew up together in the same village. I was a bit older, perhaps three months. Their house was the nearest to ours and was about three hundred yards away. Between us lay a green sea of *matoke* leaves standing oily in the haze of the sun, nudging their way heavenwards. And then a wind would sweep through them and their murmur would seem to fill the sky. When the rain fell, the chorus from those *matoke* plants was like nothing I can describe. You would feel as if life itself were spattering against and into a womb. So must the first people have thought. I am bothering you?'

Before even the boy could answer, while he was still searching for the words to tell the man that all this meant something to him, like a man who has been away a long time from home and suddenly returns in the moonlight, the old man went on.

'You town boys, what do you know? Have you uncovered the *empumumpu*, that heart-like object growing at the end of a stalk which itself is at the end of the bunch of *matoke*? And this *empumumpu* was made up of layer after layer of itself which you went on pulling off until the core lay gleaming and naked and infant-brown in your hands. And you smelled it. And it smelled like fecundity. The *matoke* garden was more than a garden of food, it was our mother.'

And he paused as the light began to fade out of the sky. And then he barked out in laughter as if deriding himself. But the past refused to relinquish him, so that even then he was only half aware of the boy. He was a long way off.

'Suddenly we were men. We became men earlier in those days. All at once the resilient soft, the unyielding, the firm, soft of the young women began to excite us. And we began to watch for their golden skin where their dresses hid them from the direct sun. And their breasts where they pressed against the sky. We were then, perhaps, about thirteen to fifteen. One day I was walking through the bush when I saw her, Nambi, Mother of Earth, or Namata or whoever, by the river, without any clothes on, washing herself. That is one of the climaxes of my life. I plucked her away bit by bit, for all the world as if she was *empumumpu*, until, like it, she lay gleaming and new to the sun. She must be dead these many years, but then she was only starting to live. And the same sun shines on. Life does not wither, does not grow old. It is we who do so.'

Again the pause as if the ghost of that long-ago day was here in the room. Furtively the dark was creeping in, subtly like a very ghost. Almost brusquely the old man pulled himself away from the image of the maiden.

'Then came the war, our final big war. There still is in my ears the lapping, sucking sound of that water against the shore. The dark trees prick the angry, heaped-up sky, and the water itself is of oil, and green-black. Whichever way you looked, the canoes full of our men stole silently, with a grim, terrible humour, upon the island. What was in our hearts then? Individually I mean, not collectively. Collectively it was courage, courage, courage. But individually, well I was thinking of my home among the *matoke* and so was my friend, as he told me later, the one who is now dead. And if a spear struck as you ran towards the enemy, you did not pull it out, for then you pulled your blood out and your life. You just ran on until afterwards, when you were looked after. My God, but it was a brave sight and an awesome sight, watching the great multitude of man, moving forever on, some of them with spears laughing out of their bodies. And you never, if you could help it, suffered a spear to come into you from the back.'

The boy thought, And here I sit pecking away at my typewriter. What manner of a man am I? What manner of men are we all nowadays? We are doomed to sterility and civilization.

'I brought away two women and a number of goats, and . . . here, reach me that spear . . . thank you . . . and this spear as well. They pulled it out of my ribs. He who is now dead, I can't, funny, isn't it, I can't bring myself to speak his name, we were together throughout.'

Slowly the ghosts rose and subsided and inside the room it was quite dark.

'We became blood brothers after that. We cut ourselves at the navel and bathed some nuts in the blood and ate the nuts and swore eternal blood-brothership. If one of us were ever in need, the other would share with him, even to a split nut. What does he mean to die now, and leave me alone? Tell me that! Do you know that he and I were yesterday the only surviving members of that victorious campaign? What else do you want to know? That we prospered and grew fat around the stomachs and sat down by the fire of an evening and re-lived that battle? That still the wind would sweep through the *matoke* and the rain spatter against and enter the womb of that garden? The Bazungu came and stayed and now they are on their way out. But all that you know. You know also that my brother has died, and now there is myself alone and I stand with the heavens against my head, like a gnarled old tree which nobody wants any more. And yet for my own sake I want to tell you something which might nail the ghost of this one who has just died.'

Little dots of yellow light had begun to wink all over the countryside and the gathering gloom was now complete. And still the old man pondered, and memories crowded in around him. The boy thought, Funny that I do not even know what he looks like. I forgot to see. And to him it was a moment of urgency, as when one has lost something very near which then attains importance and unapproachability for ever.

'Ah that's it, that's it. You know one day his wife was almost dying with fever and I had gone to see what I could do. He sat on one side of her, and I on the other. Then he lifted his eyes, which were heavy with sleep, across the shivering body of the woman, and whispered, "The thud of one's spear against an enemy's body, as it goes through him, that is a lovely sound and we've heard it, you and I." He said that, over the body of a woman he loved and whom he tended constantly for two months before she lived again, and now he is dead!'

For the first time the old man's voice cracked and the boy saw a distant light caught for a moment in the tears which coursed their way unheeded down the old cheeks. The boy rose up to go.

'Thank you sir, thank you so much.' He knew his words were inadequate. Quickly he let himself out of the house and began to walk away.

'Here,' the old man shouted behind him, and as the boy turned he saw faintly the dark length of the old man, standing in the doorway, and over beyond, far away, the twinkling lights of the city. 'Here, you've forgotten your notebook!'

Anthony M. Hokororo

A DAY OFF

The kitchen at six in the morning was bright and cheerful, but Zale was scarcely aware of that, as she washed her breakfast dishes and laid a fresh place for Abdu. She noticed, instead, the freshly laundered curtains. Everything showed what a good housekeeper she was.

Abdu gave very little thought to such things. He liked comfort, a regular routine and familiar objects where he expected to find them. He took them for granted, going off cheerfully each day to his job at the carpentry-shop, coming back at night tired, but still cheerful, accepting Zale and the dinner she served him with the same equanimity with which he took over his big chair and reading lamp, his pipe, and the *Tanganyika Standard*.

With one last look around, Zale tiptoed up to the spare-room where she had laid out her new suit the night before. She dressed quickly, put on her wide-brimmed hat with a pink rose on it and picked up her plastic handbag.

At the door of the spare room, she paused to peer through a partly open bedroom door. Abdu lay in a tangle of sheets, with one dusky arm over his head. He looked young and defenceless, with his flushed face and parted lips. Earlier in their marriage Zale could never resist kissing him awake at such moments. But now her mind registered only the fact that he was dead to the world and that he needed a shave.

Back in the kitchen, she quickly thumbed through the pages of a recent *Drum*, tore out what she wanted and thrust it into her purse. Then she scribbled a note for Abdu: 'I've decided to take a day off,' it said. 'There's rice and meat in the cupboard if I'm not back for supper. Love, Zale.' And then she slipped out the side way.

The ticket office was not open when Zale reached the station, so she had time to get her breath and tighten the elastic on her hat, which now and then slid back on her head, loosening the knot of her hair. She steadied it with extra pins, somewhat re-assured by the face which stared back at her from the mirror which she kept in her handbag.

The office now being open, Zale stepped in briskly. 'Dar, second class, please,' she said, putting her money on the counter.

The ticket clerk was Saudari. He smiled as soon as he saw her. He had earlier on pursued her but to no effect. Zale had never paid attention to men until Abdu came along.

'Goin' on a toot, baby?' he asked softly. 'In such a fairy hat, too. Somebody ought to put a flea in Abdu's ear.'

'You owe me twenty cents change,' said Zale, rather stiffly, and turned in relief at the sound of the incoming train.

Once settled, with a seat to herself, she took out the page which she had torn from *Drum* and studied the heading: SOME WOMEN GET INTO GROOVES. ARE YOU ONE OF THEM? Then she read the article for the fourth time. Such women, the article said, had only themselves to blame. For husbands had a way of just accepting unthinkingly what was done for them. That was why a wife ought to take a day off every now and then: do what she wanted to do and see what she wanted to see. The experience would be beneficial to her and to her family.

She put down the paper and sighed. The trouble was she had no idea what she wanted to do or see, at least she had not made up her mind as to what she was going to do, because for three years now her interests had been purely domestic. She was in a groove, no doubt, a household groove, and Abdu had reached the point of accepting everything without thinking, just as the article said.

At ten o'clock the train stopped at her destination. Now for the first time she felt a quiver of excitement and wished she had made a definite plan for the day. The sun shone very brightly, but the wind blew gustily from the Indian Ocean. Zale clutched her purse with one hand, and with the other steadied the big hat on her heavy hair.

From the station, she moved with the crowd across Acacia Avenue to Kariakoo, a large market place surrounded with Indian bazaars. Young people in Id El Fitr finery and with cameras swarmed in and out. The air was full of the sound of gay voices, and from the centre of the market-building could be heard trickling water running on the freshly caught fish. The smell of oriental perfumes was almost intoxicating.

Zale stood, entranced. Then suddenly, a gust of wind sent her hat spinning towards one of the rows of shops. She ran after it, conscious of the shower of hair-pins, and of the knot of hair at the back of her head slipping lower and lower. The by-standers watched her, amazed at her beauty and amused with her hat-racing. At that moment, a tall, elderly man stepped from one of the doorways, picked up the hat and held it out with a smile.

'Thank you,' murmured Zale, struggling with the remaining hair-pins, while he flicked the pink rose with an immaculate handkerchief; 'please, don't bother,' she added, in a confused state of mind.

'You're all excited, aren't you? Having a holiday from school, perhaps?'

He helped her put on the hat and then made her sit on a bench. As he sat beside her she noticed that he was not old, really. It was just because his hair had gone grey that he looked old.

The strange thing was that at that moment Zale did not at all feel disturbed by the knowledge that she was being 'picked up', something – her Mama had often told her – no girl ever permitted.

'Not from school,' she laughed. 'I'm a married woman, but I've been here only once, and – well, there's an awful lot to see in a short time. I've got to go home by the three forty-five train.'

He smiled. 'What will you see first?' he asked.

'I've got a plan,' she said firmly, and paused. 'I – I guess I'll just have to take things as they come.' It was then that she began to think she *was* being 'picked up'.

'There's the King George V's Memorial Museum,' he said, 'but it's too nice a day to spend indoors. How about the Mission Quarters, including the Cathedral?'

Her eyes widened. 'A monastery!' But, her embarrassment forgotten, she listened very eagerly while he explained that it was a kind of museum. She hesitated, but only for a second, and then off they went.

As they were coming out of the Cathedral, Zale sighed delightedly. 'I never thought that I'd be doing this,' she said.

'The nicest things are the unexpected ones,' her escort answered. 'I found that out a long time ago; so I'm often in a receptive mood. And sometimes' – his eyes twinkled – 'I even nudge at fate, speak to a stranger, buy a ticket to an unknown destination and do something I've always wanted to do and never have.'

Zale nodded quickly. Now for the first time she remembered what she had always wanted to do. 'I've always wanted to cut my hair,' she said, 'only I've never had the courage to do so.'

'Hair is sure to grow again,' he said, 'not like a finger or an ear.'

'Abdu might not like it,' murmured Zale.

'Your husband?' he asked, and, when she nodded, said, 'Well, you never can be sure about husbands until you confront them with the fact, can you?'

Zale remembered the article she had read that morning and found out that what it said was surprisingly similar to what her companion was saying.

He grew grave again. 'I'm afraid I was cross with Kate for letting her hair grow,' he said. 'But I liked it later.'

'Kate, your wife?'

He nodded.

They were now in the Rainbow Hotel where, as they talked over dessert and coffee, Zale mentioned the article that had inspired her day off, and that led to other things, so that before she knew it she had said enough about Mama and her marriage to give her listener a fair knowledge of her life. She told him that it was her Mama's sudden death five years before that had led to her marriage. She and Abdu had been living in the same house and after her Mama's death Abdu had watched her helplessly trying to keep the place in good condition. One awful night when Zale, having burnt the dinner beyond salvaging, had announced between sobs that she could not go on, and proposed that the house should be sold, Abdu had quietly objected to the proposition. This was her home, he had said, and she must stay in it. He would see to that. Then, gulping once or twice, he had asked her to marry him. He was doing well at the carpentry-shop and would be assistant master the next year. Zale had then wept in incredulous relief, grateful for his arm around her. Being married, she said, had been very great fun at first, looking after the house, making curtains and learning to cook. Abdu had shown himself to be quite a contented husband. 'But,' she concluded, 'it seems that he is too contented to – to --' She stopped, remembering the article in *Drum*.

'Husbands are always like that,' he helped her out. 'There comes that time when they take their wives for granted.'

'By the way,' he spoke again, 'you haven't told me your name. Mine is Richard, or Dick if you wish.'

'My name is Zale.'

And then his own story followed.

'Kate and I were married when we were young,' he explained, 'years ago. We lived together in our childhood. We played together. We particularly like dancing, swimming and —' He hesitated.

The change in tone perplexed Zale. Presently he told her of the accident that had changed his life. Kate had been crippled so badly while playing that she had never walked again. Her husband, of course, could not give her the care she needed. Only qualified doctors could do that. He was then working as an office boy, but, finding the wages insufficient to maintain the family, he had taken another job instead.

'It's a kaolin concern,' he said, 'and I've done well financially.'

'But being away from her,' said Zale, quite amazed at the story, 'how can you bear it?'

'I suppose it's a sort of game I play with myself,' he admitted, 'finding bits of fun and beauty here and there to take to her. Like today' – he shot a mischievous look at her – 'seeing the Mission Quarters and having luncheon with a pretty girl.'

As they went out of the hotel, the clock above the information booth struck the quarter.

'I'm afraid I must go,' said Zale, hurriedly. 'Good-bye, Mr Richard, and thank you very much for your kindness. I'll always remember how good you've been. It's been a very beautiful day to me. Only that, all of a sudden, it's – it's over.'

'Beauty, Mrs Abdu, hasn't anything to do with time,' he said. 'A great deal can be crowded into a small space, you know.'

They shook hands and parted.

As Zale walked away, the idea suggested in the article once again came before her mind, and, encouraged by Dick's words: 'You never can be sure about husbands until you confront them with the fact,' she resolved to do what she'd always wanted to to do – her hair, she must have her hair cut. There was a barber's shop on the concourse. She ran off to find it. Luckily the place was empty. 'King Saloon' was at her service, and, in a wink, her gleaming knot was lying on the floor. Experienced fingers snipped and shaped, fluffed and patted, and at 3.30 the barber stood inspecting his work with pride. She had no time to listen to compliments. She just smiled and placed a shilling on his palm.

She flew now, hat in hand, her heart pounding, afraid that she might miss the 3.45 train. With only one minute to spare she sank back in her seat and closed her eyes.

She felt as if she had been cast between two worlds, and was part of neither. Her mind still glowed with the memory of the day with Dick; and yet there was excitement in the thought that she was on her way to Abdu.

When she entered the house, there was a silence long enough to make her wonder what questions she would have to answer, what words she could possibly find to tell Abdu everything that was in her heart. But when her husband appeared, all that she could say was, 'You didn't eat your supper, Abdu, and I fixed just what you like.'

'I wasn't hungry,' he muttered. But his look of injured dignity struck a comic note, since he held a razor in his hand and one side of his face was fringed with lather. 'I heard the train coming,' he went on. 'Knew you'd be along, so —' He broke off crossly. 'Oh, the heck with it, Zale, who wants to eat alone?'

She smiled to herself, feeling suddenly older and wiser than he, for she had done what she had always wanted to do and what she had not had the courage to do before, and now he had confirmed a fundamental truth about husbands.

'O.K.,' she said, 'we'll have supper together.'

As they sat down to eat, Abdu said, in a husky voice, 'You're back and I'm glad. Only you seem different. I've missed you. Don't go away again like that without warning me. It upset me, sort of – I can't explain.'

Zale's laughter had a catch in it. 'All right, Abdu,' she said, 'I promise not to.' And she turned away to hide the new secret knowledge in her eyes.

Joseph Gatuiria

KARIUKI

The hour of midnight met with a gathering of mothers,
Their only talk – names upon names.
  'It will be my nephew,' one said,
  'No, my sister's cousin.' 'Kirahiu
  Is the name or should it be Mwangi?'
Then I heard the delicate squeal of a baby
(It is of an hour's age)
  Caused no less than a whole village to awake.
  What causes them to awake?
  And an old man comes struggling into the house.

'How are you, Kariuki?' This he whispers
To the deaf stranger of this world.
  Whereupon the 'Kariuki' begins its endless journey.
  It floats from mouth to mouth.
  'It's a boy!' 'Kariuki is born!'
  The old warrior is born again.

THE HERD

He stands on one long leg,
One scarred long leg – the other wound round it.
His thimbled muthigi is stuck in the armpit
And pegged slantwise to keep balance.
His lips twitch, his eyes stare,
His lips twitch, curled to whistle
That exclusive herdsman's quiet tune
(The tune which induces lively grazing);
It is his only occupation for years on end.
He stands lanky-legged and bare,
Positioned strategically in front of his herd
He stands –
His thimbled muthigi pegged slantwise to keep balance.

Cuthbert Khunga

TOO STRANGE NOT TO BE TRUE

'Chikanga'. It was a name fit to worry anyone – and it was certainly worrying me now. We were getting nearer and nearer to his house – in fact it would only be a short time before we would actually see it. 'Chikanga'. It was a name that mothers used to frighten their children with when they misbehaved. It was a name that conjured up fear from the bottom of the stomach. And we were actually going to his house, actually going there of our own free will. As close to him as this; the idea seemed inconceivable, seemed the utmost folly: like walking into an obvious trap that might crash down and maim one for life. When we had talked about coming here, we had been at home in our village, two hundred miles or more away. At that distance, Chikanga was only a name, the name of a man who could subdue witch-doctors, who had ultimate supernatural power. At that distance there was nothing to fear at all: those of us who knew we were innocent of practising witchcraft said that nothing but good could come from our going to see him. But now, when his spirit seemed to be reaching out to us, making our hearts beat faster, and our pulse race within us, the situation did not seem to be so clear-cut. Perhaps he might not always be right. Perhaps he would pick out one of us – perhaps it might even be me – and we would be powerless to object that we were not witch-doctors, that we had never put a spell on anyone. I was afraid. I looked around at my brothers and uncles and cousins and saw the same look on their faces. They too were afraid – we were all afraid.

We had first conceived the idea of coming to see Chikanga some months ago. We live in a small village on the shore of the Lake, a very small village indeed, for it is made up of our family alone. My uncle is head of the village and takes great care that no strangers should be allowed to come in and settle with us. He chooses the brides from one part of the family to be married to the men from another so that the links binding each part are constantly being strengthened. We are a single unit, therefore, and everything that happens in the village must be caused by the people who live there. One day my brother fell ill. It was not obvious at first what was wrong with him: he seemed to have a fever of some kind and had difficulty in breathing. After a while he got worse and we soon realized that he had *chilaso* – pneumonia. In our area we do not suffer from this disease – there is no reason why anyone should catch it, and if someone does, then it means that he has been bewitched. This set us all a problem, for although others had suddenly fallen ill in the village in the past months, it was certainly the first time for many years that we had seen *chilaso*, and if this, then what next?

Something had to be done to stop our villagers being bewitched. My uncle decided that, although he did not like to believe it, the witch must be a member of the family – it must be someone within the village, and so he called a meeting. We sat round in a circle, while my uncle called for the witch to step forward and reveal his identity. Only in this way could my brother be cured. Of course, no one stood up – not even a witch would be willing to put himself at the mercy of his clan – and neither did my uncle dare to suggest that it was any particular man: if he had been right, it would only be playing into the witch's hands. So we sat and talked, and although we all knew what the answer was, we had not the courage to come out with it. Eventually, my uncle looked slowly around the circle and in a deep and quiet voice said, 'Chikanga'. There was silence, a silence that spelt relief that the word was at last spoken, but at the same time a certain fear of what it entailed. However, we all agreed that Chikanga was our only hope, and we determined to set off for his home the next day, all of us, all the men of the

village who were fit enough to walk the long journey. We hoped
and prayed that the witch would be one of those on the journey:
if not, then our long trek would have been a waste of time. We
set off and walked and walked along the dusty roads of that part
of Nyasaland, getting ever nearer and nearer, yet always seeming
to be so far away. The days passed and we grew closer and closer
to our destination. Now we were only a short way away: and we
were already afraid of the outcome.

It was five or six minutes before we could actually see the
cluster of houses and buildings where Chikanga worked, and it
was not until we were almost upon them that we heard the steady
rhythmic pulse of a drum somewhere within. It seemed to be a
foreboding of doom, a beat that set our hearts pounding still
faster, that brought vividly into our minds horrible pictures of
what we imagined would take place within the shadows of the
main hall. There was no longer any talk, no chatter of relief that
we had arrived: only a silence within ourselves and outside,
ominous, expectant.

One of the askaris whom Chikanga employed came out to the
gate of the compound to greet us. He said that his master wel-
comed us and had been expecting us for some days. This, of
course, confirmed all our fears: that he knew us and knew we
were coming meant that he had at least some of the powers
ascribed to him. I am sure every one of us would have liked to
have turned and rushed back to our village – but no man wished
to be thought a coward, and we all followed the man to a low
building where water and food were set out for us. We were to
come to the main building in ten minutes' time. Never have ten
minutes of my life gone faster than those did, and never have
more thoughts and imaginings gone through my mind. I was
convinced that he would pick me out as the witch, convinced
that I should be the one to be blamed and punished. We washed
our dusty bodies and ate the bananas and rice put out for us.
Then, slowly, unwillingly, with my uncle in the lead, we moved
across to the hall.

It was dark and gloomy inside, and the drum we had heard
earlier could now be seen on a platform at the far end, a man

sitting behind it, his eyes closed, swaying from side to side, banging it as he moved, like an automaton. As our eyes became accustomed to the gloom we began to see that the hall was not empty, but that there were figures sitting along the wall – the askaris, their bodies painted with magic symbols, an added darkness within the all-pervading mysterious gloom. We stood in a group just inside the door, not knowing what to do, whether to go forward and sit down and wait, or to stand as if for the entrance of a king. As we faltered, the darkness in front of the drum moved, as if its spirit were emerging, and slowly, with great dignity, a man stood up in front of it. Chikanga! He was short, much younger than I had expected, in fact scarcely thirty I should think, wearing only a cloth about his waist and a cloak over his shoulders. On his head was a headdress of scarlet that hung down his sides and back, like blood pouring from a bleeding scalp. He was impressive, awe-inspiring, but not fearsome as I had expected: I began to take heart from his appearance, and felt that he would select the true witch, and that I should be safe.

He was moving unhurriedly towards us, his hands hanging by his sides, his feet moving slowly with short, smooth movements, so that he seemed to glide like a snake. He approached us and then raised both his hands in the air.

'I am Chikanga.'

My uncle bowed to him, and shuffled his feet nervously: we all tried to get behind each other so that he would not be able to look at us.

'I am Chikanga. I know why you have come. I know the name of your village, of each one of you, and the task you wish me to perform. But tell me, Khunga, tell me yourself, and I shall know the honesty of your words and the feelings in your heart.'

My uncle started as he heard his name from a complete stranger. He opened his mouth to speak but no sound came out. Then he tried again, and told Chikanga about my brother's illness and of his attempt to find out who had put the spell upon him. As he spoke Chikanga nodded his head, whether in understanding or in acknowledgement that my uncle spoke the truth, I do not know. Then he threw his hands up in the air, and we realized that he was about to find out the guilty man. The low, heavy drum began to sound faster and louder, while the askaris by the wall started beating smaller drums and singing in low voices. It was a strange, foreign music, like the wailing after the death of a man, like the jubilant cries of the head-hunters, like the noise of the thunder as it comes to destroy our fields, like the sound of the gods when they join in anger to destroy mankind. It grew louder and louder, faster and faster, and as it grew so Chikanga began to move with it, his body jerking and twisting like a woman in childbirth, like a snake that is about to strike. The noise was now deafening, no longer sound or music but only something attempting to burst our eardrums, to crush us to the ground beneath its weight. Suddenly, without warning, it came to an end, and there was an immense silence within the building: at the same time Chikanga stopped his writhing and turning, and stretching to his full height, his hands thrown back above his head, shouted, 'There is evil among us. There is one who has prayed to the mountains and to the streams, who has mixed the blood of the slain with the earth, who has moulded the charm and captured the spirit, one who has looked with the evil eye. The eyes of Chikanga are now upon him; the eyes of one who can overcome evil and death, who can cure the sick, see into the depths of the minds of men, and who can cast out the evil-doer. Let him come forward. Let him come and receive his punishment.'

There was silence, deathly and terrifying: but no one stirred. Slowly, Chikanga's eyes moved from one to another of us. Not me, I thought, please not me. His eyes looked into mine and seemed to blind me, their power was unbearable – I closed my eyes tightly, and waited. Then I heard a movement. Someone was advancing towards Chikanga; he had found the witch. I opened my eyes and saw that one of my cousins, the son of my uncle – the head man of the village – was slowly, reluctantly advancing towards Chikanga, who was himself gliding backwards towards the drum. The two of them inched forward as if bound by a cord, the one pulling with an invisible but all-powerful rope, the other unable to resist its strength.

'Here is the witch,' said Chikanga. 'Here is the man who has brought evil and disease to your village. He shall be confronted with the instruments of his foulness, and shall pay the price he deserves.'

He stooped down in front of the drum, and picked up a mirror and a needle. We all crowded forward now, relieved that we were safe, that the witch was discovered, anxious to see the punishment that would be carried out. All this time my cousin had said nothing. Now a single word fled from his lips – 'No!'

'Confess,' shouted Chikanga. 'Confess the foulness of your action.'

The words came pouring out from the poor man's lips, words spoken in terror and despair for life. He revealed how he had conjured the image of my brother into the mirror and had pierced the image with the needle. He had intended to break the needle, so that my brother would die, but had been prevented by our journey.

'So,' said Chikanga. 'You shall be punished and no longer shall you be a witch. I will purge you and your kind from our country so that there shall be no more evil, no more disease and no more death.'

Now the askaris leapt up from their drums and rushed towards my cousin. One of them produced a razor with its edge gashed and broken. My cousin was turned round with his back to the drum and bent backwards until his hair was touching the skin of its surface: there was a soft, dull booming as his head met the taut skin. Then Chikanga stepped behind the drum, and, bending forward, began to gash my cousin's face with the razor. Cut after jagged cut he made, until his face was a mass of blood, the lines running outwards from the nose, the blood dripping on to the drum. All the while the victim was screaming and shouting as the pain racked his body, writhing and struggling to free himself. It was a terrible sight and a terrible sound. One of the askaris then took some powder from a bowl and rubbed it into the cuts on my cousin's face, a whitish-grey powder that had the power of preventing a witch from ever exercising his power again. The colour would stay in the cuts for the rest of his life, and he would be ridiculed by all who met him. When they had finished, the askaris pulled the tortured body up to its feet again, and thrust it towards us. Some of the men grasped hold of him and took him out of the hall.

'He is no longer a witch,' said Chikanga. 'He no longer has any powers. Deal with him as you decide he deserves.'

We led him home with us, a pitiful, whimpering object greeted by the jeers of all who saw him. At length we reached our village; silence: no shouting, no rejoicing: my brother was already dead.

So the one-time witch was taken to our market-place. He was stretched out on the ground with pegs. The insects were grateful. His bones are still there.

Tom Chacha

ROAD TO MARA

The day was hot and humid. The air had the stillness of death. Somewhere in the distance, a bell rang. The girl listened. The shrills from the small schoolchildren had swallowed the ringing, but the girl knew it was four o'clock in the evening.

She walked slowly, almost reluctantly, from her village. Her left arm relieved the right one of the small bundle she was carrying. That bundle securely stuck under her armpit was all the property she owned in this world. Walking on that firm and dusty road was not pleasant. When an old green bus, groaning as if in great pain, appeared, the girl was happy. She waved to stop it.

'Mara?' shouted the driver.

Without answering, she got in, sat up, rather stiffly, and looked about. On her right were seated three other passengers: an old man in a stained old coat, a woman of indeterminate age and a young man. The woman smiled. The young girl, feeling rather embarrassed, returned the smile. No word passed between them.

'This must be Bena, Father,' the young man said.

'Can't you keep your eyes off the girls?' the old man whispered in a strong questioning tone. He eyed Bena; frowned; and bit his lower lip. How could a young girl like Bena travel alone without an elderly companion? The old man's eyes caught those of the woman. In the moment when their eyes met the old man knew that she was thinking the same thing as himself.

'This is one of those spoilt modern girls,' the old man seemed to be saying. 'She's probably going to be a common prostitute in the town.'

The woman, sensing the old man's thoughts, looked at Bena again. Her lips were parted; not in a smile this time, but with a mixture of pity and embarrassment. To her, Bena was a symbol of shame to all respectable women. She realized that Bena lacked something. She did not have the tribal markings on her face. Bena did not wear the iron rings on her neck. Instead she had a cross. On her arms, the tribal multi-coloured beads were replaced by a small gold watch.

'The town is ruining our young girls,' the woman whispered into the ear of the old man.

'Sure,' the old man answered, nodding his head.

It was only the young man who looked at Bena with admiration. As she got into the bus, he had watched her swaying her hips with every breath that he took. Bena was young and beautiful. Her hair was soft and coal-black. Her eyes, kind and tender. Her lips tempting, and her full sharp breasts inviting. The young man tried to smile at Bena but the smile didn't come off. He looked at Bena. Bit his fingernails. Lit a cigarette. He seemed to transmit a message through his eyes to her as if saying: 'I am with you. I know precisely what you are feeling. Don't worry. I am on your side.' His face was then as inscrutable as everybody else's.

The machine was the only thing with any life; it, at least, showed her respect. The black wheels kept on turning beneath Bena. The seat kept rocking her. And the passengers kept on harassing her with their stares. Outside, the rolling hills swept by. Soon, signs of the town began to dot the road: a board with 'Welcome to Mara' in big letters loomed up and disappeared. This encouraged Bena. It gave her confidence and hope about the friendly town.

When they reached Mara, the bus parked in front of the Mara Blue Bar and Restaurant. The passengers got out. The old man and his family stood for a second or two in complete silence, their faces now openly showing pity, contempt and embarrassment at seeing such a young girl alone in a strange town. The young man

winked at Bena and gave her a broad smile. His farewell was
well meant.

Bena stood with her eyes roving across the drab untidy town;
across the rows of *dukas*, all so quiet; across the moving people;
all so quiet too, unconcerned about anything. She transferred her
bundle to her other hand. She walked up and down the pavement. Looked at every man who passed by but she did not see
Gatimu. The crowds frightened her. The shrill cries of the boys
playing in the street annoyed her because they reminded her of
her younger brothers back home. She envied the carefree children
on the roadside. Here she was, a stranger in a lonely town.
Her man, Gatimu, did not come to meet her. Where could he
be?

The juke-box in the bar was playing a good number. The
music was soft and inviting. She went in. All eyes turned towards
her as she stepped into the bar. She held her bundle more tightly.
Her eyes were fixed on the floor.

'There is a seat this way, lady,' the waiter said in a polite but
businesslike manner.

Bena followed him obediently.

'What can I do for you, lady?' the waiter asked. She hesitated.
Her fingers found the tablecloth and she began playing with it.
After a time, she looked up. The waiter was patiently waiting for
an answer.

Reluctantly she said, 'I . . . I . . . wanted to see somebody.'

'Do you know him?'

'I was expecting him to meet me at the bus,' she said softly.

'Do you know where he stays?'

'I am a stranger here,' she said innocently, without looking at
the waiter, 'but he works on the railways,' she added.

'Then go to the railway headquarters and ask for him there.
The place is near. Once out, walk on straight right,' advised the
waiter.

Bena rose, collected her bundle and tucked it under her left
armpit. For the first time, she heard the noise the people were
making. Laughter. Music. It was all unusual to her. She threw a
glance at the waiter and said politely, 'Thank you, sir.'

She went out. Almost running. The waiter stood looking at her until she disappeared. Then he shook his head and went about his business. Bena followed the waiter's advice. A train of images passed through her mind. The crowd that pushed around her, without any apologies, did not exist. She felt bitter at heart. Beads of sweat that had collected on her forehead reminded her of tears, and her eyes filled. She let the tears flow freely as if they alone could heal the ache in her heart. Hatred burned within her. Was it her fault that she had not liked Bako? Her father had chosen him for her because Bako came from a rich family. How could he be her husband? A coward. A man who had wept at his initiation ceremony. A man who could not stand up to any challenge. The other women would taunt her at having married a coward.

'Bako a husband indeed!' she whispered to herself.

While she was debating in her mind and wondering whether she would find Gatimu in the railway headquarters, a soft hand touched her shoulders. Without looking back to see who had touched her, she shouted with joy, 'Gatimu, my love.' Sarah was surprised at this, but happy to see Bena. The two girls looked at each other without speaking. Sarah grasped Bena's hand and shook it hard.

'Bena, so you are in town!' Sarah said happily.

'Oh, I just arrived a moment ago.'

'It is a surprise. You must have come for something special?'

At this, Bena looked down shyly; wiped her face with her bare hand, then changed her bundle to her other arm.

'Bena dear, you must be tired and hungry. Let's go to that hotel across the street,' Sarah said encouragingly, leading Bena.

Bena followed obediently.

'What will you have?'

'Something cold,' Bena answered.

They were brought two *Fantas* and some cakes.

'How is everyone at home?' Sarah asked, pouring herself a drink.

'Fine,' Bena said.

'Sarah, I came to this town to look for —' She stopped, picked up her drink; put it down; took the cake, but when she was about to bite it, put that down too.

'Don't tell me you're looking for a job,' Sarah said teasingly.

Bena tried to force out a smile.

Looking at Sarah pleadingly, Bena asked, 'Tell me, where is Gatimu?'

'Surely you didn't make the whole journey to ask that,' Sarah answered innocently. Bena's moment of embarrassment and tension, a moment of hope and desire had come. Her desire to know where her secret lover was, was mounting.

'Where is he?'

'Oh, just around.'

'You mean in town? Here?'

'Oh no, he left with his wife some weeks ago for Tabora.'

The glass Bena was holding fell and broke in pieces. Her head dropped down loosely. Her fingers were trembling. She stood up to pick up the pieces of glass. 'I will do it, lady,' the waiter assured her. She covered her face with her hands. Sobbingly she told Sarah, 'I was to marry him very soon.'

Sarah felt confused. So as not to cause any embarrassment she said, 'Oh, I see!'

The waiter came. Sarah paid. She took Bena's hand politely and said, 'Let's go home and have a rest. Don't make this the end of the world.' Sarah hailed a taxi. It stopped. They moved towards it slowly, Sarah carrying Bena's bundle. 'Nyamongo quarters please,' Sarah told the taximan.

In the car, Bena felt the stabbing in her heart more severely. Her blood went cold. She could not convince herself that she was not going to Gatimu's home. She remembered the day Gatimu had told her, 'I am yours and you are mine.' Gatimu had grown fond of calling her Nancy. She now remembered the words he had said to her that night under a clear moon. The words came back to her. She could see Gatimu and herself leaning on a tree. Gatimu holding her tenderly and close to him. Her head on his wide shoulder. His voice sounding like distant music to her ears. The voice became louder and more real:

'Nancy, Nancy, are you the angel of my dreams?
Are you the beauty I see in the empty skies,
The lass I see on the face of the moon?
At night I sit and stare at the empty skies,
The moon comes and the stars dance around her.
The glow-worms sparkle her way,
As the nightingales sing in her praise.
And yet I am all alone.
Fancy, Nancy, being the moon of my world:
I'd be the nightingale to sing your praise,
The glow-worm to sparkle your paths
And the star to dance around you.'

Slowly, the musical voice of Gatimu faded away. She strained
hard to hear it but it trailed off. In that moment of darkness and
loneliness, the words of her aged mother came back to her:
'Bena, the city people are no good. You will only be happy in
the village.' Her mother had once told her so. 'How true her
prophecy!' Bena thought.

Did this mean that Bako was to marry her after all? No. Impossible. No one, nothing could shut her away from Gatimu for
ever. There must be some hope. She must go to him. She must.

'Sarah, do you think he will love me, want me and need me
while he has another woman?' Bena asked with a sob.

'Men are strange. Very strange,' Sarah said in a whisper.
Almost to herself.

Ben Mkapa

FACING A VOLCANO

Like an angry lion of the tropical jungle
The lava shoots up.
A red arrow piercing a canopy of clouds,
It threatens the endless stretch of sky.
A circling garb of hot air,
And a circling garb of humans.

A red cross on a green jeep,
A red cross on a wood shack,
A red cross on a white breast.
They stand by, grim, unshaken,
To guard this circling garb of humans.

They are all here.
Men, women; young and old,
Mystified, terrified.
They gape it in, their cameras click;
Later, removed in space and time,
They will vent an endless chime:
'Is it not wonderful?'
A boy and a girl, but a few hours met,
Their backs to the volcano, they face the camera;
He wants a souvenir.
'Is it not wonderful?'
A beautiful girl, and behind – a beautiful monster.

A big truck unloads its cargo.
Majestic, springy, the cargo swells the circling garb of humans.
These are guards, of men against other men.
The army, of course! They too missed the red lion.
No, no, this is no enemy; just a 'glorious sight.'
And the red tongue lashes out.
But it won't lick the sky;
It won't lick these men – there are other tongues!

What thoughts do they all have? What feelings?
As the eruption's bowel of lost time hurls
The granitic deluge of suppressed earth which
Apace invades forlorn man and crop, and
Imposes a reign of barrenness;
What thoughts do they all have? What stirs them?
Fear, awe,
Man helpless in contest with nature.
He cannot harness this; he cannot explore it.

What a fire! it surpasses hell.
But the clergyman is not here;
He has known a hell fire; he doesn't have to see it.
It is better imaged in the cloister, in the pulpit
Better described.
Nothing real, this heat, and dust, and fire.
It makes no souls repent.

They work at calculations,
Scientists and seismographs.
It defies them all, this tongue of fire, this fierce fiasco of rock and
    dust;
It defies time, this fiery testimony of nature.
Ruthless, devastating, defiant,
An angry arrow of fire.

James Ngugi

THE RETURN

The road was long. Whenever he took a step forward, little clouds of dust rose, whirled angrily behind him, and then slowly settled again. Meanwhile a thin train of dust was left in the air, moving like smoke. He walked on, however, unmindful of the dust and ground under his feet. Yet with every step he seemed more and more conscious of the hardness and apparent animosity of the road. Not that he looked down; on the contrary, he looked straight ahead as if he would, any time now, see a familiar object that would hail him as a friend and tell him that he was near home. But the road stretched on.

He made quick, springing steps, his left hand dangling freely by the side of his once white coat, now torn and worn out. His right hand, bent at the elbow, held on to a string which supported a small bundle on his slightly drooping back. The bundle, well wrapped with a cotton cloth that had once been printed with red flowers now faded out, swung from side to side in harmony with the rhythm of his steps. The bundle held the bitterness and hardships of the years spent in detention camps. Now and then he looked at the sun on its homeward journey. Sometimes he darted quick side-glances at the small hedged strips of land which, with their sickly-looking crops, maize, beans, and so forth, appeared much as everything else did – unfriendly. The whole country was dull and seemed weary. To Kamau, this was nothing new. He remembered that, even before the Mau Mau emergency, the over-tilled Kikuyu holdings wore

C

haggard looks in contrast to the sprawling green fields in the
settled area.

A path branched to the left. He hesitated for a moment and
then seemed to make up his mind. For the first time, his eyes
brightened a little as he went along the path that would take
him down the valley and then to the village. At last home was
near and, with that realization, the faraway look of a weary
traveller seemed to desert him for a while. The valley and the
vegetation along it were in deep contrast with the surrounding
country. For here green bush and trees thrived. This could only
mean one thing: Honia river still flowed. He quickened his
steps as if he could scarcely believe this to be true till he had
actually set his eyes on the river. It was there; it still flowed.
Honia, where so often he had taken a bath, plunging stark
naked into its cool living water, warmed his heart as he watched
its serpentine movement round the rocks and heard its slight
murmurs. A painful exhilaration passed through him and for a
moment he longed for those days. He sighed. Perhaps the river
would not remember in his hardened features that same boy to
whom the river-side world had meant everything. Yet as he
approached Honia, he felt more akin to it than he had felt to
anything else since his release.

A group of women were drawing water. He felt excited, for he
could recognize one or two from his ridge. There was the middle-
aged Wanjiku, whose deaf son had been killed by the Security
Forces just before he himself was arrested. She had always been
a darling of the village, having a smile for everyone and food for
all. Would they receive him? Would they give him a 'hero's
welcome'? He thought so. Had he not always been a favourite
all along the Ridge? And had he not fought for the land? He
wanted to run and shout: 'Here I am. I have come back to you.'
But he desisted. He was a man.

'Is it well with you?' A few voices responded. The other
women, with tired and worn features, looked at him mutely as if
his greeting was of no consequence. Why! Had he been so long
in the camp? His spirits were damped as he feebly asked: 'Do
you not remember me?' Again they looked at him. They stared

at him with cold, hard looks; like everything else, they seemed
to be deliberately refusing to know or own him. At last Wanjiku
recognized him. But there was neither warmth nor enthusiasm
in her voice as she said, 'O, is it you, Kamau? We thought
you —' She did not continue. Only now he noticed something
else – surprise? fear? He could not tell. He saw their quick
glances dart at him and he knew for certain that a secret from
which he was excluded bound them together.

'Perhaps I am no longer one of them!' he bitterly reflected.
But they told him of the new Village. The old Village of scattered
huts spread thinly over the Ridge was no more.

He left them, feeling embittered and cheated. The old Village
had not even waited for him. And suddenly he felt a strong
nostalgia for his old home, friends and surroundings. He thought
of his father, mother and – and — He dared not think about
her. But for all that, Muthoni, just as she had been in the old
days, came back to his mind. His heart beat faster. A pang of
desire passed through him. He quickened his step. He forgot the
village women as he remembered his wife. For he had stayed
with her for a mere two weeks; then he had been swept away by
the Forces. Like many others, he had been hurriedly screened
and then taken to detention – without trial. And all that time he
had thought of nothing but the village and his beautiful woman.

The others had been like him. They had talked of nothing but
their homes. One day he was working next to another detainee
from Muranga. Suddenly the detainee, Njoroge, stopped breaking stones. He sighed heavily. His worn-out eyes had a faraway
look.

'What's wrong, man? What's the matter with you?' Kamau
asked.

'It is my wife. I left her expecting a baby. I have no idea what
has happened to her.'

Another detainee put in: 'For me, I left my woman with a
baby. She had just delivered. We were all happy. But on the same
day, I was arrested . . .'

And so they went on. All of them longed for one day – the day
of their return home. Then life would begin anew.

Kamau himself had left his wife without a child. He had not
even finished paying the bride-price. But now he would go, seek
work in Nairobi, and pay off the remainder to Muthoni's parents.
Life would indeed begin anew. They would have a son and bring
him up in their own home. With these prospects before his eyes,
he quickened his steps. He wanted to run – no, fly to hasten his
return. He was now nearing the top of the hill. He wished he
could suddenly meet his brothers and sisters. Would they ask
him questions? He would, at any rate, not tell them all – all about
his sufferings, all his work on the roads and in the quarries with
an askari always nearby ready to kick him if he relaxed. Yes. He
had suffered many humiliations, and he had not resisted. Was
there any need? But his soul and all the vigour of his manhood
had rebelled and bled with rage and bitterness.

One day these wazungu would go!

One day his people would be free! Then, then – he did not
know what he would do. However, he bitterly assured himself
no one would ever flout his manhood again.

He mounted the hill and then stopped. The whole plain lay
below. The new Village was before him – rows and rows of
compact mud huts, crouching on the plain under the fast-vanish-
ing sun. Dark blue smoke curled upwards from various huts,
and formed a kind of dark mist that hovered over the village.
Altogether it was very impressive and for a time he forgot his
old home. Beyond, the deep, blood-red sinking sun sent out
finger-like streaks of light that thinned outwards and mingled
with the grey mist shrouding the distant hills.

In the village, he moved from street to street, meeting new
faces. He inquired. He found his home. He stopped at the
entrance to the yard and breathed hard and full. This was the
moment of his return home. His father sat huddled up on a
three-legged stool. He was now very aged and Kamau pitied
the old man. But he had been spared – yes, spared to see his
son's return —

'Father!'

The old man did not answer. He just looked at Kamau with
strange vacant eyes. Kamau was impatient. He felt annoyed and

irritated. Did he not see him? Would he behave like the women Kamau had met at the river?

In the street, naked and half-naked children were playing, throwing dust at one another. The sun had already set and it looked as if there would be moonlight.

'Father, don't you remember me?' Hope was sinking in him. He felt tired. Then all of a sudden he saw his father tremble like a leaf. He saw him stare with unbelieving eyes. Fear was discernible in those eyes. His mother came, and his brothers too. They crowded around him. His aged mother clung to him and sobbed hard.

'I knew my son would come. I knew he was not dead.'

'Why, who told you I was dead?'

'That Karanja, son of Njogu.'

And then Kamau understood. He understood his trembling father. He understood the women at the river. But one thing puzzled him: he had never been in the same detention camp with Karanja. Anyway he had come back. He wanted now to see Muthoni. Why had she not come out? He wanted to shout, 'I have come. Muthoni; I am here.' He looked around. His mother understood him. She quickly darted a glance at her man and then simply said:

'Muthoni is gone.'

Kamau felt something cold settle in his stomach. He looked at the village and the dullness of the land he had passed through seemed to blind his vision. He wanted to ask many questions but he dared not. He could not yet believe that Muthoni had gone. But he knew by the look of the women at the river, by the look of his parents, that she was gone.

'She was a good daughter to us,' his mother was explaining. 'She waited for you and patiently bore all the ills of the land. Then Karanja came and said that you were dead. Your father believed him. She believed him too and keened for a month. Karanja constantly paid us visits. He was of your rika, you know. Then she got a child. We would have kept her. But where is the land? Where is the food? Ever since land consolidation, our last security was taken away. We let Karanja go with her. Other

women have done worse – gone to town. Here only the infirm
and the old have been left.'

He was not listening; the coldness in his stomach slowly
changed to bitterness. It would choke him. He felt bitter against
all, all the people including his father and mother. They had
betrayed him. They had leagued against him, and Karanja had
always been his rival. Five years was admittedly not a short time.
But why did she go? Why did they allow her to go? He wanted
to speak. Yes, speak and denounce everything – the women at
the river, the village and the people who dwelt there. But he
would not. This thing was choking him.

'You – you gave my own away?' he whispered.

'Listen, child, child —'

The big yellow moon dominated the eastern horizon. It was
like a great eye, watching two grief-stricken parents as they
helplessly watched their son slip away in bitterness.

He stood on the bank of Honia River. He gazed fixedly at the
river without actually seeing it. He was seeing his hopes being
dashed on the ground instead. The river moved swiftly, making
the same ceaseless murmurs. In the forest the crickets and other
insects kept up an incessant buzz. And above, the moon shone
in all her brightness. His heart began to thaw. He tried to remove
his coat, and the small bundle he had held on to so firmly fell. It
rolled down the bank and before Kamau knew what was happening, it was floating swiftly down the river. For a time he was
shocked and wanted to retrieve it. What would he show his —
Oh, then he remembered. Had he forgotten so soon? His wife
had gone. And all the little things that had so strangely reminded
him of her and that he had guarded all those years, had gone! He
did not know why, but somehow he felt relieved. Warmth began
to rise in his heart. He felt as if he would dance the magic of the
night, the ritual of the moon and the river. All thoughts of
drowning himself dispersed. Life was still sweet. He began to put
on his coat, all the time murmuring to himself, 'Why should she
have waited for me? Why should all the changes have waited for
my return?'

'My son!'

He quickly turned round. There, standing and looking resplendent under the bright moon, was his aged mother. For the first time he saw sorrow and untold hardships written on her wrinkled face. He felt like weeping, yes, weeping like a woman. She had all the time followed him. He looked at her and forgot all about himself.

'Mother!' It was a softened voice full of emotion. He went towards her and took her by the arm. 'Let's go home!' he murmured again. This was truly his 'return', and as he peered into the future, as he became aware of the beauty of life in spite of its hardships, he could see no possibility of his going away again.

THE VILLAGE PRIEST

Joshua, the village priest, watched the gathering black clouds and muttered one word – 'Rain'. It was almost a whisper, spoken so quietly that a man a yard away would not have heard it. He was standing on a raised piece of ground looking thoughtfully at the clouds and the country around. Behind him stood a tin-roofed rectangular building from which thick black smoke was beginning to issue, showing that the woman of the house had already come from the shamba and was now preparing the evening meal. This was his house – the only one of its kind along the ridge, and beyond. The rest were mud-walled, grass-thatched round huts that were scattered all over the place. From these also black smoke was beginning to curl upwards.

Joshua knew that in most of the huts the inmates had been sleeping with contracting, wrinkled stomachs, having eaten nothing or very little. He had seen such cases in the past months during his rounds of comforting the hungry and the suffering, promising them that God would in time bring rain. For the drought had been serious, and had lasted many months, so that

crops in the fields had sickened, while some had dried up altogether. Cows and goats were so thin that they could hardly give
enough milk.

If it rained now it would be a blessing for everyone, and
perhaps crops would revive and grow and all would be well.
The dry anxious looks on the faces of mothers and fathers would
disappear. Again he looked at the darkening clouds and slowly
the old man retraced his steps to the house.

Soon it began to rain! Menacing thunderstorms boomed in
the heavens and the white spots of lightning flashed across with
a sharpness and fury that frightened him. Standing near a window, the priest, his horse-shoe-shaped bald head lined with short
grey bristles of hair, watched the slanting raindrops striking the
hard ground and wetting it. 'Jehovah! He has won!' the priest
muttered breathlessly. He felt cheated, bitter and angry. For he
knew that the coming of rain so soon after the morning sacrifice
would be nothing but a victory for the rain-maker at whose
request a black ram had been sacrificed. Yes. This was the culmination of their long fight, their long struggle and rivalry in
Makuyu village.

Makuyu was an isolated little place. Even the nearest missionary station was some fifty-five miles off – quite a long way
in a country without roads. It was in fact one of the last areas to
be seriously affected by the coming of the white missionaries,
farmers and administrators. And so while the rest of the country
had already seen the rain-maker, the witch-doctor and black-
magic workers being challenged by Christianity, this place had
remained pretty well under the power and guidance of the rain-
maker.

The challenge and rivalry here began when the Rev. Livingstone of Thabaini Mission made a visit and initiated Joshua into
this new mystery – the new religion. The white man's God was
said to be all powerful, all seeing, the only one God, creator of
everything. And the rain-maker (he was also a magic-worker) had
denounced his rivals when he saw how many people had been
converted by Joshua into this new faith. He had felt angry and
tried to persuade people not to follow Joshua. He threatened

them with plague and death. But nothing had happened. The
rain-maker had even threatened Joshua.

But Joshua had not minded. Why should he? Had he not
received an assurance from Livingstone that this new God would
be with him 'always, even unto the end of the earth?'

Then the drought had come. And all the time Joshua told the
village that there would be rain. And all the time he prayed over
and over again for it to come down. Nothing had happened.
The rain-maker said the drought was the anger of the old God.
He, the rain-maker, was the only person who could intercede for
the people. Today under the old sacred tree – Mugumo – a black
ram, without any blemish, was sacrificed. Now it had rained!
All that morning Joshua had prayed, asking God not to send
rain on that particular day. Please God, my God, do not bring
rain today. Please God, my God, let me defeat the rain-maker
and your name shall be glorified. But in spite of his entreaties it
had rained.

He was puzzled; he could not understand it. And through the
evening his forehead remained furrowed. He spoke to no one.
He even went to bed and forgot to conduct the evening prayer
with his family. In bed he thought and thought about the
new God. If only Livingstone had stayed! All might have
been well. He would have read from the black book and then
prayed to his God and the rain-maker would not have won.
A week later Livingstone would have prayed for rain at a public
meeting. Then everyone would have believed and Joshua
would have remained the undisputed spiritual authority in
Makuyu.

A thought occurred to him; so staggering was it that for a
time he could neither move nor breathe as he lay on his bed
woven with rope and bamboo poles! He ought to have thought
of this, ought to have known it. The new God belonged to the
whiteman and could therefore listen to none but a man with a
white skin. Everybody had his own God. The Masai had theirs.
The Agikuyu had theirs. He trembled. He seemed to understand
everything. Some gods were stronger than others. Even Livingstone probably knew this. Perhaps he feared the Gdo of Agikuyu.

That is why he had gone away and had not appeared all the time the drought had continued.

What shall I do? What shall I do? Then his way became clear. A sacrifice had been performed that day. Early in the morning, he would go to the sacred tree and there make peace with his tribal god.

The morning was dark and chilly. The first cock had already crowed. Joshua had just put on a big raincoat over his usual clothes. He trudged quietly across the courtyard.

The dark silhouette of the house and the barn beside it seemed watchful and ominous. He felt afraid. But his mind was fixed. Down the long path, to the distant forest, to the sacred tree, and there make peace with the god of his tribe. The birds were up and singing their usual morning songs, the prelude to dawn. To Joshua they had a doleful note and they seemed to be singing about him. The huge old tree stood where it had always been, even long before Joshua was born. The tree too looked at once mysterious and ominous. It was here that sacrifices to God were made under the direction of the tribal elders and the medicine-man. Joshua made his way through the surrounding dry bush and to the foot of the tree. But how did one make peace with God? He had no sacrificial ram. He had nothing.

'God of Agikuyu, God of my tribe . . .'; he stopped. It sounded too unreal. False. He seemed to be speaking to himself. Joshua began again. 'God of . . .' It was a small crackling laugh and the crack of a broken twig that interrupted him. He felt frightened and quickly turned his head. There, standing and looking at him maliciously, was the rain-maker. He laughed again, a menacing dry laugh but full of triumph.

'Hmm! So the fox comes to the lion's den. Ha! Ha! So Joshua comes to make peace. Ha! Ha! Ha! . . .' Joshua did not wait to hear more. He quickly moved away from the dumb tree, away from the rain-maker. It was not fear. He no longer feared the tree, nor the rain-maker. He no longer feared their power, for somehow it had all seemed to him false as he spoke to the tree. It was not even the feeling of defeat. It was something else, worse . . . shame. It was a feeling of utter hollowness and hope-lessness that can come only to a strong-willed person who has sacrificed his convictions. Shame made him move more quickly. Shame made him look neither to the left nor to the right as he made his way back, in the break of day.

The journey was long. The path was muddy. But he did not mind. He saw nothing, felt nothing. Only this *thing*, this hollow feeling of shame and hatred of self. For, had he not sacrificed his convictions, his faith, under the old tree? 'What would Living-stone say to me now?' he kept on murmuring to himself. Living-stone would rebuke him again. He would think him unworthy. He had once rebuked him when he had found Joshua quietly sipping just a little beer to quench his thirst. He had another time warned him when he had found Joshua beating his wife because she had not promptly obeyed him.

'This is not the way a man of God acts,' Livingstone told him in a slow sorrowful tone. Yes. No-one could understand Living-stone. At one time he would be unreasonably stern and im-perious, and at another time he would be sorrowful. And as he looked at you with his blue sunken eyes, his head covered with a thick-rimmed sun helmet, you could never divine his attitude. Joshua was now sure that Livingstone would think him quite useless and unworthy to be a leader. He thought of himself so, too.

The sun had already appeared in the east when Joshua finally reached his home. He stood outside and surveyed the whole ridge and countryside. Suddenly he felt like running away and never preaching again. He was so deep in thought that he did not seem to see the anxious, excited countenance of his wife as she came out to announce that 'somebody', a visitor, had called and was waiting for him in the house.

Who could it be? These women. They would never tell anyone who a visitor was, but must always talk of somebody. He did not really feel like seeing anyone for he felt transparent through and through. Could it be the witch-doctor? He shuddered to think of it. Could it be one of his flock? And what would he tell him after he himself had betrayed the trust? He was not worthy to be a priest. If I saw Livingstone today I would ask him to give me up. Then I would go away from here.

He entered and then stopped. For there sitting on a three-legged Gikuyu stool was no other than Livingstone himself. Livingstone, tired and worn out after a whole night's journey, looked up at Joshua. But Joshua was not seeing him. He was seeing something else.

He was seeing the altar on which he had sacrificed his convictions. He was seeing the rain-maker in whose magic and power he no longer believed.

Run away, Joshua! But he did not move.

Run away, Joshua! But he went nearer Livingstone.

Do not tell him then! But he told him everything. And all the time Joshua had not dared to lift his head. He kept it down. And as he confessed, even this sense of utter hollowness and shame, he felt as if strength was ebbing from his legs. He was sinking down, down . . . ; he leaned more firmly against the wall, with his eyes still bent to the ground. Livingstone had not spoken a word. There was complete silence. Joshua could hear his own heart beating, tom-tom, tom-tom. He was waiting for Livingstone to stand up and go, after upbraiding him and telling him how unworthy of his calling he had been.

Cautiously Joshua lifted his eyes. He met the full smiling face of Livingstone. Joshua was never more surprised in his life. The old sternness and apparent hardness of Livingstone was no longer in his eyes but only a softened, sympathetic understanding of a man who seemed to be looking at a new Joshua. Joshua could not understand this and his heart beat faster and more loudly.

Suddenly the two men met in a hand-shake, a hand-shake that made Joshua's heart and love go out to Livingstone. They mutely looked at one another; none broke the silence that settled about them.

When Joshua's wife came in and found Livingstone standing she was taken aback.

'Why! going away so soon?'

The old village priest glanced at his wife and then at Livingstone. 'Not yet!' he said.

His wife went back to the other room wondering what had happened to her husband, the old village priest. When she came back a few minutes later she found them both busy talking about the problems of Makuyu now that the rain had come and the menacing drought was over.

GONE WITH THE DROUGHT

At long last, I also came to believe that she was mad. It was natural. For my mother said that she was mad. My brothers and sisters maintained that she was mad. And everybody in the village seemed to be of the same opinion. Not that the old woman ever did anything really eccentric as mad people do. She never talked much. But sometimes she would fall a victim to uncontrollable paroxysms of laughter for no apparent reason. Perhaps they said so because she stared at people hard as if she was seeing something beyond them. She had sharp glittering eyes whose 'liveness' stood in deep contrast to her wrinkled, emaciated body. But there was something in that woman's eyes that somehow suggested mystery and knowledge, and right from the beginning shook my belief in her madness. What was the something and where was it? It may have been in her, or in the way she looked at people, or simply in the way she postured and carried herself. It may have been in any one of these, or in all of them at once.

I had occasion to mention this woman and my observations about her to my father. He just looked at me and then quietly said, 'Perhaps it is sorrow. This burning sun, this merciless drought . . . running into our heads making us turn white and mad!'

I didn't then know why he said this. I still believe that he was not answering my question but rather was speaking his thoughts aloud. But he was right – I mean, right about 'whiteness'.

For the whole country appeared white – the whiteness of death.

From ridge up to ridge the neat little shambas stood bare. The once short and beautiful hedges – the product of land consolidation and the pride of Gikuyu farmers in our district, were dry and powdered with dust. Even the old mugumo-tree that stood just below our village, and which was never dry, lost its leaves and its greenness – the living greenness that had always scorned short-lived droughts. Many people had forecast doom. Weather-prophets and witch-doctors – for some still remain in our village though with diminished power – were consulted by a few people and all forecast doom.

Radio boomed. And 'the weather forecast for the next twenty-four hours', formerly an item of news of interest only to would-be travellers, became news of first importance to everyone. Yes. Perhaps those people at K.B.S. and the Met. Department were watching, using their magic instruments for telling weather. But men and women in our village watched the clouds with their eyes and waited. Every day I saw my father's four wives and other women in the village go to the shamba. They just sat and talked, but actually they were waiting for the hour, the great hour when God would bring rain. Little children who used to play in the streets, the dusty streets of our new village, had stopped and all waited, watching, hoping.

Many people went hungry. We were lucky in our home – unlike most families – because one of my brothers worked in Nairobi and another one at Limuru.

That remark by my father set me thinking more seriously about the old woman. At the end of the month, when my mother bought some yams and njahi beans at the market, I stole some and in the evening went about looking for the mud hut that belonged to the woman. I found it. It was in the very heart of the village. That was my first meeting with the woman. I have gone there many times. Yet that evening still remains the most vivid of all. I found her huddled together in a dark corner while the dying embers of a few pieces of wood in the fireplace flickered slightly, setting grotesque shadows over the mud walls. I was frightened and wanted to run away. I did not. I called her 'grandmother' – though I don't think she was really so old as to warrant that – and gave her the yams. She looked at them and then at me. Her eyes brightened a little. Then she lowered her face and began wailing.

'I thought it was "him" come back to me,' she sobbingly said. And then: 'Oh, the drought has destroyed me!'

I could not bear the sight and ran away quickly, wondering if my father had known it all. Perhaps she was mad.

A week later, she told me about 'him'. Words could never recreate the sombre atmosphere prevailing in that darkish hut as she incoherently told me all about her life-long struggle with the droughts.

As I have said, we had all, for months on end, sat and watched, waiting for the rain. The night before the day when the first few drops of rain fell was marked with an unusual solitude and weariness infecting everybody. There was no noise in the streets. The woman, watching by the side of her only son, heard nothing. She just sat on a three-legged Gikuyu stool and watched the dark face of the boy as he wriggled in agony on the narrow bed near the fireplace. When the dying fire occasionally flickered, it revealed a dark face now turned white. Ghostly shadows flitted across the walls as if mocking the lone watcher by the bedside. And the boy kept on asking,

'Do you think I'll die, Mother?' She did not know what to say or do. She could only hope and pray. And yet the pleading voice of the hungry boy kept on insisting, 'Mother, I don't want to die.' But the mother looked on helplessly. She felt as if her strength and will had left her. And again the accusing voice: 'Mother, give me something to eat.' Of course he did not know, could not know, that the woman had nothing, had finished her last ounce of flour. She had already decided not to trouble her neighbours again for they had sustained her for more than two months. Perhaps they had also drained their resources. Yet the boy kept on looking reproachingly at her as if he would accuse her of being without mercy.

What could a woman without her man do? She had lost him

during the Emergency, killed not by Mau Mau or the Government forces, but poisoned at a beer-drinking party. At least that is what people said, just because it had been such a sudden death. He was not now there to help her watch over the boy. To her this night in 1961 was so different from such another night in the 40's when two of her sons died one after the other because of drought and hunger. That was during the 'Famine of Cassava' as it was called because people ate flour made from cassava. Then her man had been with her to bear one part of the grief. Now alone. It seemed so unfair to her. Was it a curse in the family? She thought so, for she herself would never have been born but for the lucky fact that her mother had been saved from such another famine by missionaries. That was just before the real advent of the whitemen. Ruraya Famine (the Famine of England) was the most serious famine to have ever faced the Gikuyu tribe. Her grandmother and grandfather had died and only she, from their family, had been saved. Yes. All the menace of droughts came to her as she watched the accusing, pleading face of the boy. Why was it only her? Why not other women? This her only child, got very late in life.

She left the hut and went to the headman of the village. Apparently he had nothing. And he seemed not to understand her. Or to understand that droughts could actually kill. He thought her son was suffering from his old illnesses which had always attacked him. Of course she had thought of this too. Her son had always been an ailing child. But she had never taken him to the hospital. Even now she would not. No, no, not even the hospital would take him from her. She preferred doing everything for him, straining herself for the invalid. And this time she knew it was hunger that was killing him. The headman told her that the D.O. these days rationed out food – part of the Famine Relief Scheme in the drought-stricken areas. Why had she not heard of this earlier? That night she slept, but not too well for the invalid kept on asking, 'Shall I be well?'

The queue at the D.O.'s place was long. She took her ration and began trudging home with a heavy heart. She did not enter but sat outside, strength ebbing from her knees. And women and men with strange faces streamed from her hut without speaking to her. But there was no need. She knew that her son was gone and would never return.

The old woman never once looked at me as she told me all this. Now she looked up and continued, 'I am an old woman now. The sun has set on my only child; the drought has taken him. It is the will of God.' She looked down again and poked the dying fire.

I rose up to go. She had told me the story brokenly yet in words that certainly belonged to no mad woman. And that night (it was Sunday or Saturday) I went home wondering why some people were born to suffer and endure so much misery.

I last talked to the old woman about two or three weeks ago. I cannot remember well as I have a bad memory. Now it has rained. In fact it has been raining for about a week, though just thin showers. Women are busy planting. Hope for all is mounting.

Real torrential rain began yesterday. It set in early. Such rain had not been witnessed for years. I went to the old woman's hut with a gift, this time not of yams and beans, but of sweet potatoes. I opened the door and found her huddled up in her usual corner. The fire was out. Only a flickering yellow flame of a lighted lantern lingered on. I spoke to her. She slightly raised her head. In the waning cold light, she looked white. She opened her eyes a little. Their usual unearthly brightness was intensified a thousand times. Only there was something else in them. Not sadness. But a hovering spot of joy, or exultation, as if she had found something long-lost, long-sought. She tried to smile, but there was something unearthly, something almost diabolical and ugly in it. She let out words, weakly, speaking not directly to me, but actually declaring aloud her satisfaction, or relief.

'I see them all now. All of them waiting for me at the gate. And I am going . . .'

Then she bent down again. She never spoke any more. Almost at once the struggling lantern light went out, but not before I had seen in a corner all my gifts; the food had never been touched but had been stored there. I went out.

The rain had stopped. Along the streets, through the open doors, I could see lighted fires flickering, and hear people chattering and laughing.

At home we were all present. My father was there. My mother had already finished cooking. My brothers and sisters chattered on, about the rain and the drought that was now over. My father was unusually quiet and rather thoughtful. I also was quiet. I did not join in the talk, for my mind was still on the 'mad' woman and my untouched gifts of food. I was just wondering if she too had gone with the drought and hunger. Just then, one of my brothers mentioned the woman and made a jocular remark about her madness. I stood up and glared at him.

'Mad indeed,' I almost screamed. And everybody stared at me in startled fear. All of them, that is, except my father, who kept on looking at the same place.

THE FIG TREE

Great complicated, nude fig-tree, stemless flower-mash,
Floweringly naked in flesh, and giving off hues of life.

There was a flower that flowered inward, womb-ward;
Now there is a fruit like a ripe womb.

                                        D. H. LAWRENCE

Mukami stood at the door; slowly and sorrowfully she turned her head and looked at the hearth. A momentary hesitation. The smouldering fire and the small stool by the fire-side seemed to be calling her back. No. She had made up her mind. She must go. With a smooth oiled upper-garment pulled tightly over her otherwise bare head, and then falling over her slim and youthful shoulders, she plunged into the lone and savage darkness.

All was quiet and a sort of magic pervaded the air. Yet she felt it threatening. She felt awed by the immensity of the darkness – unseeing, unfeeling – that enveloped her. Quickly she moved across the courtyard she knew so well, fearing to make the slightest sound. The courtyard, the four huts that belonged to her airu, the silhouette of her man's hut and even her own, seemed to have joined together in one eternal chorus of mute condemnation of her action.

'You are leaving your man. Come back!' they pleaded in their silence of pitying contempt. Defiantly she crossed the courtyard and took the path that led down to the left gate. Slowly, she opened the gate and then shut it. She stood a moment, and in that second Mukami realized that with the shutting of the gate, she had shut off a part of her existence. Tears were imminent as with a heavy heart she turned her back on her rightful place and began to move.

But where was she going? She did not know and she did not very much care. All she wanted was to escape and go. Go. Go anywhere – Masailand or Ukambani. She wanted to get away from the hearth, the courtyard, the huts and the people, away from everything that reminded her of Muhoroini Ridge and all its inhabitants. She would go and never return to him, her husb – No! not her husband, but the man who wanted to kill her, who would have crushed her soul. He could no longer be her husband, though he was the very same man she had so much admired. How she loathed him.

Thoughts of him came into her head like a mighty flood. Her young married life came back to her; Muthoga, her husband, a self-made man with four wives but with a reputation for treating them harshly; her father's reluctance to trust her into his hands and her dogged refusal to listen to his remonstrances. For Muthoga had completely cast a spell on her. She wanted him, longed to join the retinue of his wives and children. Indeed, since her initiation she had secretly but resolutely admired this man – his gait, his dancing, and above all his bass voice and athletic figure. Everything around him suggested mystery and power. And the courting had been short and strange. She could still remember the throbbing of her heart, his broad smile and her hesitant acceptance of a string of oyster-shells as a marriage token. This was followed by beer-drinking and the customary bride-price.

But people could not believe it and many young warriors whose offers she had brushed aside looked at her with scorn and resentment. 'Ah! Such youth and beauty to be sacrificed to an old man.' Many a one believed and in whispers declared that she was bewitched. Indeed she was: her whole heart had gone to this man.

No less memorable and sensational to her was the day they had carried her to this man's hut, a new hut that had been especially put up for her. She was going to the shamba when, to her surprise, three men approached her, apparently from no-where. Then she knew. They were coming for her. She ought to have known, to have prepared herself for this. Her wedding day had come. Unceremoniously they swept her off the ground, and for a moment she was really afraid, and was putting up a real struggle to free herself from the firm yet gentle hands of the three men who were carrying her shoulder-high. And the men! the men! They completely ignored her frenzied struggles. One of them had the cheek to pinch her, 'just to keep her quiet', as he carelessly remarked to one of his companions. The pinch shocked her in a strange manner, a very pleasantly strange manner. She ceased struggling and for the first time she noticed she was riding shoulder-high on top of the soft seed-filled millet fingers which stroked her feet and sides as the men carried her. She felt really happy, but suddenly realized that she must keen all the way to her husband's home, must continue keening for a whole week.

The first season: all his love and attention lavished on her. And, as in her youth, she became a target of jealousy and resentment from the other wives. A strong opposition soon grew. Oh, women. Why could they not allow her to enjoy what they had enjoyed for years – his love? She could still recall how one of them, the eldest, had been beaten for refusing to let Mukami take fire from her hut. This ended the battle of words and deeds.

It was now a mute struggle. Mukami hardened towards them. She did not mind their insolence and aloofness in which they had managed to enlist the sympathy of the whole village. But why should she mind? Had not the fulfilment of her dream, ambition, life and all, been realized in this man?

Two seasons, three seasons, and the world she knew began to change. She had no child.

> A *thata!* A barren woman!
> No child to seal the bond between him and her,
> No child to dote on, hug and scold!
> No child to perpetuate the gone spirits of
> Her man's ancestors and her father's blood.

She was defeated. She knew it. The others knew it. They whispered and smiled. Oh how their oblique smiles of insolence and pride pierced her! But she had nothing to fear. Let them be victorious. She had still got her man.

And then without warning the man began to change, and in time completely shunned her company and hut, confining himself more to his thingira. She felt embittered and sought him. Her heart bled for him yet found him not. Muthoga, the warrior, the farmer, the dancer, had recovered his old hard-heartedness which had been temporarily subdued by her, and he began to beat her. He had found her quarrelling with the eldest wife, and all his accumulated fury, resentment and frustration seemed to find an outlet as he beat her. The beating; the crowd that watched and never helped! But that was a preamble to such torture and misery that it almost resulted in her death that very morning. He had called on her early and without warning or explanation had beaten her so much that he left her for dead. She had not screamed – she had accepted her lot. And as she lay on the ground thinking it was now the end, it dawned on her that perhaps the others had been suffering as much because of her. Yes! she could see them being beaten and crying for mercy. But she resolutely refused to let such beating and misgivings subdue her will. She must conquer; and with that realization she had quickly made up her mind. This was no place for her. Neither could she return to her place of birth to face her dear old considerate father again. She could not bear the shame.

The cold night breeze brought her to her present condition. Tears, long suppressed, flowed down her cheeks as she hurried down the path that wound through the bush, down the valley and through the forest. It was so dark that she could hardly pick her way through the labyrinth of thorn and bush. The murmuring stream, the quiet trees that surrounded her, did these sympathize with her or did they join with the kraal in silent denouncement of her action?

She followed the stream, and then crossed it at its lowest point where there were two or three stones on which she could step. She was still too embittered, too grieved to notice her dangerous surroundings. For was this not the place where the dead were thrown? where the spirits of the dead hovered through the air, intermingling with trees, molesting strangers and intruders? She was angry with the world, her husband, but with herself. Could she have been in the wrong all the time? Was this the price she must pay for her selfish grabbing of the man's soul? But she had also sacrificed her own youth and beauty for his sake. More tears and anguish.

Oh spirits of the dead, come for me!
Oh Murungu, god of Gikuyu and Mumbi,
Who dwells on high Kerinyaga, yet is everywhere,
Why don't you release me from misery?
Dear Mother Earth, why don't you open and swallow me up
Even as you had swallowed Gumba – the Gumba who
    disappeared under mikongoe roots?

She invoked the spirits of the living and the dead to come and carry her off, never to be seen again.

Suddenly, as if in answer to her invocations, she heard a distant, mournful sound, pathetic yet real. The wind began to blow wildly and the last star that had so strangely comforted her vanished. She was alone in the gloom of the forest! Something cold and lifeless touched her. She jumped and at last did what the beating could not make her do – she screamed. The whole forest

echoed with her scream. Naked fear now gripped her; she shook
all over. And she realized that she was not alone. Here and there
she saw a thousand eyes that glowed intermittently along the
stream, while to and fro she felt herself being pushed by many
invisible hands. The sight and the sudden realization that she
was in the land of ghosts, alone, and far from home, left her
chilled. She could not feel, think or cry. It was fate – the will of
Murungu. Lower and lower she sank onto the ground as the last
traces of strength ebbed from her body. This was the end, the
culmination of her dream and ambition. But it was so ironic.
She did not really want to die. Life was sweet. She only
wanted a chance to start life anew – a life of giving and not only of
receiving.

   Her misery was not at an end for even as she lay on the ground,
and even as the owl and the hyena cried in the distance, the wind
blew harder, and the mournful sound grew louder and nearer;
and it began to rain. The earth looked as if it would crack and
open beneath her.

   But even as the lightning came and the thunder struck, she
espied a tree in the distance – a huge tree it was, with the bush
gently but reverently bowing all around the trunk. And she
knew; she knew, without telling that this was the tree – the
sacred fig-tree that is called *Mukuyu* – the altar of the all-seeing
Murungu. 'Here at last is a place of sanctuary,' she thought.

   She ran, defying the rain, the thunder and the ghosts. Her
husband and the people of Muhoroini Ridge vanished into in-
significance. The load that had weighed upon her heart seemed
to be lifted as she ran through the thorny bush, knocking
against the trees, falling and standing up. Her impotence was
gone. Her worries were gone. Her one object was to reach the
fig-tree. It was a matter of life and death – a battle for life. There
under the sacred fig-tree she would find sanctuary and peace.
There Mukami would meet her God, Murungu, the God of her
tribe. So she ran depite her physical weakness. And she could feel
a pleasant burning inside that made her womb dance. Now she
was near the place of sanctuary, the altar of the most High, the
place of salvation. So towards the altar she ran, no, not running

but flying; at least her soul must have been flying. For she felt as light as a feather. At last she reached the place, panting and breathless.

And the rain went on falling. But she did not hear. She had lain asleep under the protecting arms of God's tree. The spell was on her again.

Mukami woke up with a start. What! Nobody? Surely that had been Mumbi, who standing beside her husband Gikuyu had touched her – a gentle touch that went right through her body. No, she must have been dreaming. What a strange beautiful dream. And Mumbi had said, 'I am the mother of the tribe.' She looked around. Darkness still. And there was the ancient tree, strong, unageing. How many secrets must you have held?

'I must go home. Go back to my husband and my tribe.' It was a new Mukami, humble yet full of hope who said this. Then she fell asleep again. The spell . . .

The sun was rising in the east and the rich yellowish streaks of light filtered through the forest to where Mukami was sitting, leaning against the tree. And as the straying streaks of light touched her skin, she felt a tickling sensation that went right through her body. Blood thawed in her veins and oh! she felt warm – so very warm, happy and light. Her soul danced and her womb answered. And then she knew – knew that she was pregnant, had been pregnant for some time.

As Mukami stood up ready to go, she stared with unseeing eyes into space, while tears of deep gratitude and humility trickled down her face. Her eyes looked beyond the forest, beyond the stream, as if they were seeing something, something hidden in the distant future. And she saw the people of Muhoroini, her *airu* and her man, strong, unageing, standing amongst them. That was her rightful place, there beside her husband amongst the other wives. They must unite and support the tribe, giving it new life. Was Mumbi watching?

Far into the distance, a cow lowed. Mukami stirred from her reverie.

'I must go.' She began to move. And the fig-tree still stood, mute, huge and mysterious.

David Rubadiri

AN AFRICAN THUNDERSTORM

From the west
Clouds come hurrying with the wind
– turning
– sharply turning
Here and there
Like a plague of locusts
– whirling
Tossing things up on its tail
– hurrying
Like a madman chasing nothing.

Pregnant
They gather to perch on hills
Like dark sinister wings,
The wind whistles furiously by
And trees bend to let it pass.

In the villages
Screams of delighted children
Toss and turn
In the din of whirling wind,
– women
Babies clinging on their backs
– dart about
– in and out
– madly

Clothes
Wave like tattered flags
Flying off
To expose dangling breasts
As jaggered blinding flashes
rumble
tremble
and crack!
Amidst the smell of fired smoke
In the rumbling belly of the storm.

STANLEY MEETS MUTESA

Such a time of it they had
The heat of the day
The chill of the night
And the mosquitoes
That day and night
Trailed the march bound for a kingdom.

The thin weary line of porters
With tattered dirty rags
To cover their backs
The battered bulky chests
Perched on sweating shaven heads;
The sun fierce and scorching
Its rise their hope
And its fall their rest;
Sweat dripped off their bodies
Whilst clouds of flies
Clung in thick clumps
On their sweat-scented backs,
Such was the march
And the hot season just breaking

Each day a weary pony dropped
Left for the vultures on the plains,
Each afternoon a human skeleton collapsed
Left for the hyenas on the plains,
But the march trudged on
Its khaki leader in front
He the spirit that inspired
He the beacon of hope.

Then came the afternoon of a long march
A hot and hungry march
The Nile and the Nyanza
Like a grown tadpole
Lay azure
Across the green countryside,
They had arrived in the promised land.

The march leapt on
Chaunting, panting
Like young gazelles to a waterhole.
Hearts beat faster
Loads felt lighter
Cool soft water
Lapt their sore feet,
No more
The dread of hungry hyenas
Or the burning heat of sand on feet
Only tales of valour,
Song, laughter and dance
When at Mutesa's court
In the evening
Fires are lit.

The village looks on behind banana groves
Children peer with round eyes behind reed fences,
That was the welcome –
No women to wail a song
Or drums to greet the white ambassador,

Only a few silent nods
From a few aged faces
Only a rumbling peel of drums
To summon Mutesa's court to parley;
You see there were rumours
Tales and rumours at court
Rumours and tales round the countryside:
That was expected
Mutesa was worried.

The reed gate is flung open
The crowd watches in silence
But only a moment's silence
A silence of assessment –
The tall dark tyrant steps forward
He towers over the thin bearded whiteman
Then grabbing his lean white hand
Manages to whisper
'Mtu mweupe karibu'
White man you are welcome,
The gate of reeds closes behind them
And the west is let in.

A NEGRO LABOURER IN LIVERPOOL

I passed him
Slouching in dark backhouse pavement
– head bowed
– taut
– haggard
– and worn
A dark shadow
Amidst dark shadows.

I stared;
Our eyes met
But on his dark negro face
No sunny smile
– no hope
Or a longing for a hope promised.
Only
– the quick cowed dart of eyes
Piercing through impassive crowds
Searching longingly
– for a face
That might flicker understanding.

This is him,
The Negro labourer in Liverpool
That from his motherland
With new hope
Sought for an identity
– grappled
To clutch the fire of manhood
In the land of the free.

Will the sun
That greeted his nativity
Again ever shine?
– maybe
– but not here
Here his hope
– the shovel
His fulfilment
– resignation.

G. K. Gicogo

THE SWORD OF NJERU

Centuries have passed, for this happened when the ages were nearer to the beginning and gods were more familiar. Close to the towering peak of Mount Kenya there lived a very eccentric man, a rare specimen of the human race. As the legend tells us, he was famous all over Kikuyuland, not because of his courage or strength, but for a skill which in most cases is no blessing but a curse. He was a thief by profession, ever ready to thrust his long fingers into his neighbours' property; he would not hesitate to relieve any passer-by of his 'burden'.

One sunny afternoon he went into a neighbouring sugar-cane plantation with a fixed determination to try his luck at stealing some sugar-canes so that he might brew some beer for his father-in-law who was likely to visit him some days later. Njeru had very little difficulty in fulfilling his wicked plans; he cut down a good number of canes and tied them into a bundle so that he could carry them easily. Then he thought that it would be a very good idea if he chewed one of the canes before he left the place.

This day, however, Njeru was unfortunate, for he had hardly consumed half of the cane when his alert ears detected the rattling of leaves as somebody moved through the plantation. Certainly, this was the owner of the farm; so, with the least possible delay, Njeru showed a clean pair of heels; he ran as fast as his legs could carry him. Aware of his loss, the new-comer ran after him but Njeru was nowhere to be seen; he had gone where the dead crabs go.

Unfortunately for him, Njeru did not think of snatching up his sword as he left; there it lay beside the sugar-cane bundle. The disappointed 'policeman' carried everything away thinking that if anyone turned up to claim the sword, he could be accused of theft. It was late in the evening when Njeru retraced his steps to the farm in the hope of recovering his property; but it was nowhere to be seen. Do not imagine that he had the courage to go and claim it; but he was not the man to despair at the first failure.

At that time the Akikuyu believed that God had His head-quarters on the top of Mount Kenya, and that when He was hun-gry, or when He had a declaration to make, He would make use of the biggest tree in the area and from there He would proclaim His demands. Njeru was not ignorant in these matters. Close to his village was a huge fig-tree from which God was said to com-municate with the people. Njeru decided to take the place of God, and to make his unquestionable demands known from this tree.

Early the following morning Njeru climbed into the upper branches and waited for the best opportunity to present himself, making sure that not a soul could see him in his hiding-place. As the sun rose, he saw the wife of the farmer leave the house: this was his long-awaited opportunity. In a low, awe-inspiring voice, he began singing as follows:

> 'Let Njeru's sword be restored;
> The sugar-canes are to be included too;
> In addition there should be some tobacco;
> It is I, God, who command this.'

When the woman heard the song, she hurried back into the house and informed her husband of God's manifesto. On gaining this intelligence, the husband was dumbfounded; he ran to his field, cut down a fresh bundle of sugar-canes, and on returning home, he took the sword and some tobacco and started on his way to the 'altar'. Politeness and good manners were essential because he was going into the presence of God. He was very careful not to look upwards lest he should chance to see God the

Almighty. He left his load at the foot of the tree and ran home without having the courage to turn his head. He locked himself and the family in his hut to leave the Rain-Giver time to come down the tree and inspect the offerings.

Meanwhile, Njeru could not help smiling to himself when he contemplated his own cleverness. He descended the tree and hurried everything away before anybody could see him. I wish you could picture the happiness that filled the farmer's heart when, an hour later, he saw that his gift, like that of Abel, had been accepted. He said within himself: 'I am blessed.'

Valentine Eyakuze

KAMARA, THE BUTCHER KING

For seven months the harpers of Ndoro had not sung the beauty and grace of Kengeleire, the king's favourite wife. She had retired from public life, and her maids had been asked to join the retinue of other court ladies. It was an open secret that she was with child, and that the court diviner had foretold the birth of a boy – the heir-apparent to the throne. According to tribal custom it was taboo for Kengeleire to see a woman throughout her confinement, except the old court midwife whose prescriptions and orders she obeyed without question. The day finally came; the king's representative was invited to witness the birth of the prince, and the Diviner's word came true. The baby prince, holding an ear of corn – the symbol of royal descent – was brought before the court and named Kamara after his grand-father.

Kamara grew into a handsome but intractable youth. As heir-apparent he could never see his father. He was king in his own establishment, sanctioned to hold an imitation court with young men of his age. He would sometimes take part in their activities, such as tending cattle in the fields all day, for the fun of it. He could not understand, however, why cattle were so greedy that even after an all-day meal of the juiciest meadow grass they would still reach out for anything green on their way home. He resolved to cure them of this when he became king.

Another problem which exercised his proud mind was the size of his future kingdom. He considered it too small for his

D

mighty self and drew up plans for its expansion. He undertook to reorganize his father's army in readiness to realize his day-dreams, and as he was a popular prince he easily attracted the younger generation into the army. He would drill with his youthful soldiers all day and complain of the time being too short at sunset, which came against his will. The sun was one of those rare objects that did not seem to observe his wishes, and so he vowed to subdue it when he became King Kamara.

He was supervising one of those day-long drills when he was called to his father's death-bed. King Kuga's last breath was squeezed out by the royal strangler, for custom sanctioned the quick relief of the dying king. Kamara kissed his dead father, received the regalia and turned to those present. They sank on their knees in recognition of the sovereignty of Kamara the Second.

A youth of indomitable will and great physical strength, Kamara at once set about implementing his resolutions and fulfil-ling his vows. He decided to start by curing his cattle of their insatiable greed for food. He ordered all the cows and oxen from the royal pens to be herded under his supervision for seven days and nights. At the end of this period they were being driven home when he noticed that even now they were reaching out for more leaves. Enraged by this signal defeat so early in his reign, he ordered a carnival in which cattle would be killed on Naga Hill until their blood flowed into Mizo, a river one mile below the summit. Whole carcases were roasted and eaten, and there was wild merriment on the first day. But the royal herds had all been killed before their blood had flowed half a mile. Cattle from neighbouring villages were commandeered and slaughtered, while men were appointed to the fatal office of reporting to the king the distance covered by the bloody stream. This employ-ment was ill-fated because every messenger who brought news that the stream had not yet reached Mizo contributed his own blood to the flow.

The carnival turned into a massacre, but the king's mighty order, like the law of the Medes and Persians, could not be repealed. But at last on the third day the one fortunate bearer of this office delivered the great news: the waters of the Mizo were crimson with blood! Kamara had earned the title of the Butcher-King.

Next on the programme of his undertakings came the subjection of the sun. He convinced himself that if he brought the sun under his control, this would serve a double purpose. He could then make it rise and set at will, and he might order it not to shine on the surrounding kingdoms which would finally beg for light and recognize his sovereignty. He gathered all the blacksmiths of his kingdom together and when they were assembled he sprang on them the order to build an iron tower to reach up to the sky and bring the sun down to him. The blacksmiths realized the folly of the king's command, but who dared cross the will of the mighty prince? They set to work, therefore, and all the male population of the kingdom was conscripted to dig up iron ore, smelt it and feed it into the smithy that was turning out the rungs of the colossal Ladder of Ndoro – for that was the kingdom over which Kamara reigned.

One day the king had gone to inspect the progress of this tower when it began swaying in the wind and then collapsed with the loudest crash that had ever been or ever will be heard, killing every living thing in its way. The mighty Kamara, who believed he could rule over the sun and stars, the prince who dreamt of reaping laurels in every field, was frustrated.

After recovering from this great defeat he realized that he had been attempting to do what he could never do. He turned to an achievement that would mask his failures – the construction of a palace that was to be the envy of kings and the jewel of Ndoro. He built it of polished ivory and ebony and thatched it with black banana fibre. The completed palace was a symphony of black and white. The king now announced the date of the grand house-warming feast. Wishing to fit into the white and black pattern of the 'Ivory and Ebony Palace', the king had the raw hide of a white bull stitched tightly on to his body, and at the grand festival he appeared on the royal platform to great advantage and in perfect harmony with the walls of the palace. As it dried, however, the hide shrank, and the tight-fitting neck began to suffocate the king so that he suffered greatly. Before the idea of soaking the king in water to loosen the skin was hit upon, he was gasping for breath. The royal strangler was summoned to perform his office, and he obligingly pressed life out of the dying king.

So Kamara did not live to make good his failures. The magnificent palace stood many years after his death, the sun still rose and set at will, and cattle ate as much grass as they chose. Kamara had attempted to tame nature but it had tamed him instead. He had massacred cattle: a white bull avenged them with its skin.

So goes the story of the Butcher-King, told to me by my grandfather at the fireside, in return for blowing on the embers that warmed his ageing frame. He in his turn had heard it from his grandfather, who had eaten of the roasted carcases at the cattle carnival, smelted iron for the 'Ladder of Ndoro', and felled the ebony trees to build the 'Ivory and Ebony Palace'.

Michael Kaggwa

TO...

And so you have gone,
Gone your usual paradoxical ways
Meaning to return,
But never returning;
And you have gone,
Gone with only one smiling look behind
Leaving me here to scribble this verse.

Jonathan Kariara

'UNTO US A CHILD IS BORN'

The red cock crowed once, twice; the third time it was accompanied by a chorus of chattering sparrows. On coming out of his hut and looking to the east, Kariuki was delighted by the golden arrows which streaked the sky. As he looked, a large red ball appeared, then surged up the sky through the scanty clouds; solemnly dispersing the invisible archers whose arrows had fretted the path of the rising sun. The birds were heard no more, the ascending sun had hushed them. All was calm, unbearably calm.

Then suddenly there were bells, ringing in all directions. These were not the soothing bells of cattle feeding in distant fields but the pealing bells of human creation, symbols as it were of the human spirit which refuses to be calmed or dominated. This was a Christmas Day, the day when Christians would rejoice, never looking up to the sky to see the pitiless ball of fire which even at that height communicated its malignity in piercing shafts of white sunlight.

This would be a quiet day for Kariuki, who, not being a Christian, had to spend the day alone. Though not a Christian, Kariuki got on tolerably well with his neighbours. They were Christians, but not all the time. Generally they were just neighbours, all concerned with the same problems, the same interests. They all had their likes and dislikes, but even here they all agreed that Mumbi, the headman's wife, was the village gossip, and that Kiguta, their old chief, was a suckling lioness. They regarded Kariuki with admiration and a little suspicion. They had tried to make him a Christian, not because they felt very strongly about the new faith, but because it was neighbourly to become one. They admired him for sticking to the old faith because most of them still felt that it represented the best way of life. They were suspicious of his strength of mind which could stand against the limping missionary who had undauntedly approached and converted – as they all wanted to believe – the old chief. Perhaps the men envied him this independence and tended to cover their envy with a slight contempt, and repeated to their wives that he had medicines and charms which he used against all persuasion. But Kariuki was a useful member of the society. He rose early, and therefore provided fire for all the village women. More important still, he was a brave warrior, always the first to plunge his spear into the angry body of a marauding lion. The neighbours resented his tall figure which had the best of their virtues and none of their faults. If some of them had at times wished him ill luck, none of them had ever thought of inflicting it on him themselves.

Today he would not go herding. The cattle had been forced to feed all the previous night so that they could be shut in during the day to give the men a chance to go to the celebrations across the valley at the chief's big kraal. He could hear the villagers now toiling noisily on the other side of the valley, with their cries of Hosanna coming across to him distinctly. It was about noon now, and Kariuki looked up at the midday sun of December, and wondered how people could make merry when everything else drooped and gasped for breath in the sweltering sun. He did not understand the joy felt; manifestation of this joy, therefore, made the participants seem ridiculous and impious. He thought with regret and frustration of the tribal worship his village had given up. At this time of the year they would have been offering a lamb to the relentless sun-god, praying for rain to come. Blood would flow and the lamb would cease its movements, and the angry god would be propitiated. The Christians talked of birth and hope for new life, but Kariuki could not see these things when he looked out of the dark low doorway of his hut across the breathless plains of savanna grass.

Perhaps it was this lack of occupation, perhaps it was the loneliness in the village or, more likely still, perhaps it was the fact that Nambi, his secret love, was now dancing with all the other village youth across the valley, that made Kariuki feel unsettled all day. He had been restless, and towards nightfall a tight feeling had been gathering in his chest as though a terrible thing was about to happen. By sunset he felt he must do something. He would go across the valley to the place where the rest of the villagers were. No, that would never do, for had he not refused again and again to have anything to do with the new religion? But he must do something, and he wanted very much to be with human beings, to hear human voices, not Christians, but speaking human beings! Above all he felt he wanted to see Nambi.

The sun was fast sinking from the sky, its blood-red glow gradually merging into the engulfing darkness which was swiftly approaching. Yes, he must go, even to the revelling Christians. Only the valley to cross and he would be reunited with humanity.

He was running now, not knowing why he ran. The valley must be crossed, he must feel safe in the company of the others.

He was at the bottom of the valley when he saw two figures, a man and a woman. The woman was Nambi, the black-eyed beauty, daughter of the chief. He loved her, but her father did not approve of this love. He knew she loved him, though she never dared show it. Had he not often met her at the well with her maids? and had he not seen how she always lifted her eyes to him, though never daring to raise those drooping eyelashes? And there she was now, talking to the man her father had chosen for her. Kariuki felt weak at the knees and sat on a stone at his feet; for a moment he was unconscious of all surrounding objects, transfixed there on the stone, with only the profiled figure of the girl standing against the red sunset before him. And then he saw it all. There was a short struggle, the girl wanting to go past the man, and the man detaining her with a rough hand. Kariuki tried to move but could not. The man then pulled a dagger from its sheath and for a moment held it in the air. The dagger reflected the red evening sun on its shiny surface, making a streak of red like a thunderbolt. For a moment it was reared in the air, then gathering fury it drove with mad determination into the girl's uplifted bosom. The blow staggered her so that she now faced Kariuki, her outstretched arms forming against the red background the image of the cross he had often seen in the 'Christians' House'. He was to see it all. He saw the man look this way and that, and then gather a few leaves near by, wipe his knife on them and throw them on the fallen body. The man sheathed his knife and again looked about him, then with a determined face he directed his course into the red eye of the sun, which was now very swiftly sinking into the surrounding darkness. The man's movements were easy, stalking over the grass like the red stags Kariuki had often seen on the level plains of Kikuyuland. The sun went down, swallowing the man.

Kariuki was not to live long enough to know what happened after that. When he came to himself people were pulling at him madly, trying to tear him from the fallen figure of the girl. They called him murderer, but he did not know why. They tore his clothes; he did not struggle. They beat him; he did not murmur a word. Always before him was the figure with the outstretched arms, bathed in a red light. He *knew* she loved him.

In the village that night they cast lots, and decided on burning the murderer. The custom is, that if a man commits a murder, he is tied to the door-post of his hut and the hut is set on fire from behind. The fire gradually eats up the hut, finally swallowing the man. Kariuki knew that the drama which had been enacted in the valley would be repeated on the hill. He too would stand against the red glow, and would die thinking of that figure with the outstretched arms. He would not complain; he could not. He was not even sure that the tall graceful figure he had seen stalking over the grassland was Nambi's intended husband. He associated it with the red eye of the sinking sun, and almost felt convinced that this was the wrathful messenger from the malicious sun-god, sent to demand the blood that was no more shed for the god. Who then could he accuse of having killed the girl? All he felt he could do was to gather up what little strength they had left him, and in the final moment die with outstretched arms like Nambi, his love, had done.

The hut is on fire now. They have tied the man to the door-post. Kariuki, who is a tall man, seems to tower over the hut. They are quiet now. In the final moment their fury against this supposed murderer is spent. They stand back, a silent audience, to watch the drama before them. The fire gathers swiftly around the erect figure, leaving it for a moment tall and black against the red glow. The flames dance nearer and nearer, they lick his shoulders, sending a shiver through his frame. But he does not cower before the fire, he gathers his strength and with out-stretched arms stands taller than ever. The onlookers see his action and shrink within themselves, gathering closer to one another. The women whimper and steal away, not waiting to see the end. The men stand transfixed, with bowed heads, until finally there is the crash, and they know the end has come.

Why do they all stand sorrowing, they who, in their crude manner, have been trying to administer justice? Do they also remember another drama two thousand years ago, these people who in the morning cried Hosanna, and at nightfall have shed innocent blood?

THE INITIATION

Mirashi sat brooding by the bamboo bed, quietly watching the rise and fall of his son's chest. His mouth was hard set; his look was anxious and strained. He was watching the sleeping youth, Mlaponi, his only son. The boy had been very sick; today was the fortieth day since he had undergone circumcision. Mlaponi slept quietly. The bed was woven with rope and bamboo poles. A blanket protected his body against the hardness. His head rested on a heap of rags and bark cloth put over the short tree trunk which raised the mat at one end. They were in an isolated hut of poles and grass thatch, about a hundred paces away from the main camp.

Under the blanket wrapped round him, one could feel the frail

wasted body of Mlaponi. He had been tender and weak from
birth and the past weeks had made him thinner. The boy reminded his father of the plucked doves he used to roast with
other boys in the fields, with his thin chest and the ribs spreading
out like bare boughs on a dry tree. His body was feverishly hot,
just like one of those birds. His wound had not yet healed, and
possibly would never heal. All the other candidates for the year's
initiation had recovered within the usual six weeks. But Mlaponi
had got worse every day. There was only another week to go.
The camp would close down, and the candidates, fit in body, and
mature in manhood, would return home to be respected as men
of the tribe. It was a disgrace and an ill omen for a candidate to
return home with the wound half healed. It predicted death in
the family.

Mirashi was thinking of the day the boy was born. That was
before his journey to Lindi, how many years was it? Twenty.
He had gone to cook for Mr Allison. Mr Allison had gone back
'home', the name he always used when referring to his place of
birth. He had inherited two things from the white man, a new
religion and the desire to decide for himself. But he had not been
given the chance to decide for himself when he came back to his
birth-place. Mlaponi had to undergo initiation in the tribal
manner . . . Mirashi wanted to be a Makua, an ageing member
of a venerable tribe. And why not? Who were his parents? Had
not his father's people been always Wamakua of Mpeta from
time immemorial? But he was different. And he knew it. Mlaponi,
however, had to undergo the ceremony. 'I, Mirashi, desired it!'
he insistently went on, showing his doubts even in his insistence.

He was interrupted in these thoughts by the waking of his son.
Mlaponi was perspiring; he tossed about, wailing fitfully.
'Father, am I going to get well? Is there no help, Father?' he
asked repeatedly. When he was not asking these questions, he
kept looking accusingly at his father with eyes that spoke openly:
'You must know of a way of releasing me from this pain. You
must!' There the father sat, helpless with suffering, seeing no
way out, none but that suggested by the elders. Why must he
always come up against the elders? He had had great difficulty

persuading them to let Mlaponi be initiated, so sure were they that Mlaponi was too weak and young. How hostile they had been when he refused to accompany them to the communal ceremony of planting herbs on the outskirts of the camp and on the circumcision ground.

Was there no way out, indeed? He knew the answer too well. Mirashi could not bear to reflect. He stepped out of the hut and walked towards the camp. Like a hawk he surveyed the elders grouped round evening fires, seeking out Omanya. The elders watched him with apparent interest. There was a secret understanding among them, a tie that excluded Mirashi. Had they not always said that somehow something would go wrong in Mirashi's household? And had they not taken care to tell the older relatives that Mirashi had proved obstinate? It is not that they enjoyed the fact that their fears had been realized; rather they pitifully patronized him. They had confirmed by consulting the witch-doctor that Mirashi's bad luck had been brought about by the ill-will and magical practice of Mlaponi's maternal aunt. They had advised Mirashi to accede to custom and make a supplication to the woman to ease the pain in the boy. But he had refused, becoming blind and dumb to any suggestion that he would ever ask help from the woman. How, humiliate himself before the woman who had thought her sister had not married well by marrying him. No! But now he began to feel he would have to go – to save the boy.

Presently Mirashi spotted Omanya in one of the groups and called him out. He asked him to look after Mlaponi, promising to come back soon.

'But where are you going?' asked Omanya, surprised. 'Oh, nowhere,' Mirashi answered carelessly. He turned round, indifferent to the elders' stares and purposefully trod through the grass to the top of the hill. His eyes were fixed, seeing nothing. But he had his destination clearly in his mind, the tall baobab-tree near his house. He went on stiffly, feeling alone and tired.

At last he reached the tree and climbed it, branch by branch. He turned towards the woman's house and let out the plaint: 'Leave my son alone. Oh, leave him alone. He is not the one who has wronged you! Why don't you harm the one who is responsible for the wrongs done to you? Oh, let him come back home safely. Let him come and die in his mother's eyes! Spare my child; leave my son to me; spare him!!'

He came down the tree feeling ashamed. The shame almost drove him mad, so that he was running, shouting, 'It will never be repeated again.' He had hoped against hope that the sacrifice of his convictions and integrity would lead to the recovery of his son. But now, as he slowly made his way back, he knew he had only shamed himself. He reached the bottom of the valley and stopped. He realized that even at this moment, Mlaponi might be dead. This apprehension grew.

He was almost running now, to get back to the boy. At the top of the hill he stopped, breathless. Before him spread the blurred lights of the camp. He looked back to the village, to the baobab-tree, the scene of his shame. The fires in front of the houses in the village danced before his eyes, mockingly. And before him was always the pleading face of the boy, and the maddening question always in his ears – 'Is there no help, Father?' 'No, no help for you, Mlaponi; your ritual must be the agony of ritual carried to the extreme, even the agony of death. It is me you have got to save, from fear and pride, from wanting to graft the old to the new.' It dawned on him then; that his son had been weak all the time, that it was his pride that had forced his son to go through an ordeal for which he had lost his life. Already he felt his son was dead.

Wearily he began to descend. And then it was as though out of the silence a piercing cry was directed to his ears, the cry of a fox. 'It means death,' he told himself. He felt strangely calm, and relaxing his steps he walked easily as a countryman walks when enjoying a well-earned hour of ease. He went to one of the camp fires, and chose a seat among the elders. He sat easily among them, letting the warmth of the fire knit him into the group. He could even crack jokes about Kagasi, a young man of twenty-five who had the incurable habit of roasting sweet potatoes wherever he was, whenever there was a fire handy. Quiet little jokes which drove fear into the people so that several were already squirming in their seats and clearing imaginary obstructions in their throats. 'You know that the boy is dead,' Mirashi said quietly. They looked at him as if to say that they knew, but how could he know? He read this in their eyes and in a tired small voice which strived to be normal said, 'Oh yes, I know. Or is it not so?' tugging the shoulder of the man next to him in pathetic little movements. 'Ay, it is so,' said most of the neighbours.

'You must then help me to carry him to the village – no, not to the village. It would not be right. His wound never healed; it would bring ill-luck to the villagers. No, not to the village, but to the top of the hill, where we must dig a grave for him in the night, before the women wake to make their noises. And neighbours, you can come to my house on the third day from this, and you will find ready the beer and foods that our funeral rites dictate. I will not be home that day, but I am sure you will not miss me. I will see to there being enough beer.'

On the third day, in the village could be heard sounds of much rejoicing, a lot of noisy drumming and thick hoarse shouts of a people who have drunk freely from a beer-gourd. Mirashi had apparently fulfilled his promise to the people. But he was not among them. After the burial in the night he had gone home, ordered the feast that was to take place in three days and had immediately started on a journey to Lindi. He did not find Mr Allison in the growing mission, but that did not matter. A language already existed between Mirashi and these white men, a language that could handle day-to-day experiences, even death, with ease. The rites that had not been fulfilled in his village were fulfilled at Lindi, and so on the third day Mirashi was on his way home again, carrying a small wooden cross hidden in his clothes. He climbed to the top of the hill, stumbling a little over the newly turned clods at the graveside. He dug a small hole, inserted the cross at the head of the grave. He felt physically tired. Moving a few yards away he lay himself down on the warm grass to wait for the rejoicings in the village to stop. The ritual was over. The cross was not high; it could never be seen from the village. But it might be seen by a few who by chance might stray into the hills, perhaps by a shepherd looking after his sheep in the fields.

AGE AND EXPERIENCE

Sitting down
An old man is like a rock, rough hewn,
Which a god shaped –
Shaped here and scooped there
With sharp eagerness.

Standing
And supporting himself with a crook,
The weakness creeps out at the knee,
And the old man now is like a dragon-fly
At the painful moment of birth.

We are born, and grow.
Quietly, imperceptibly, the process unfolds,
Of a baby growing to a boy, a boy to a man.
And then suddenly we realize
That what we were we no longer are.

Then the drama starts
– It's a fight fitful and feverous –
Of shifting ourselves into this guise and that,
Touching, tasting, testing –
Staining the purity of youth.

But relief comes with experience,
Experience, the pegs of pain
Piercing to the formless mass
Of the turmoil inside man.
Now the soul is born, but gone too is the fire
Which would have inspired it.

So man falls back
To the patterned repetition of traditions.
And so sitting down he looks rock-strong,
But standing is the broken pitcher.

THE DREAM OF AFRICA

I lay the other night and dreamt
That we were all being glazed
With a white clay of foreign education,
And it was stifling, stifling the sleeping blackman
Inside there.
Making him fester.
Liberating worms of thought, books, boots.
O, o, what's gnawing me there?
Pinching me at the seat of the brain?
We were given books, and they
Pinched what they touched,
Wrought us to great perplexity
Of selves we did not understand,
Did not want to understand.
'We must educate you, you see.'
Doctor, what ails me, what ails –
(The bottled ale I took the other night to forget.)
The ready-made pill prescription
For a slight mental maladjustment
Due to – due to – that's not for us to know:
It is the knowing doctor's secret.
'Business, you see.'
So we glibly take it, the pill,
Which smoothes the pain and smoothes the nerves,
And sends the disease to sleep.
And to rot. This white precipitate
Of an age-old decay of a foreign culture
Africa gaped for, glazed her sons with,
To prepare them for an international role in the future.
Will it be the pearl in the oyster shell,
Or mere rottenness?

James McCarthy

THE TALISMAN

'I hate him,' thought Onyango.

'I hate him! I hate him!' re-echoed his footsteps on the ochre *murram*, still damp from the morning dew. Even the birds in the jacaranda trees seemed to sense his hate as they shrieked their early song . . . or were they, too, laughing raucously at the bitterness in Onyango's heart? He picked up a stone and threw it violently into the foliage. The birds rose in a screaming, mocking cloud and disappeared behind the banana patch. Onyango shifted his bundle, tied loosely in a red kerchief, and appearing pathetically inadequate, and for the hundredth time brooded over the events of the past twenty-four hours.

It had all started yesterday morning, that vital morning when he had decided to take the talisman to school. After breakfast he had stolen surreptitiously to his bedroom, and from beneath the faded blanket had taken his most treasured possession. It was a curious object. A monkey's tail, pierced at the end by a metallic ring which glittered in the pale light, and from which was suspended a small clump of blue feathers. Glancing quickly at the door, he had stuffed the vital charm inside his shirt and set off cheerful, even on examination day – for had not this very charm succeeded in the past? He thought gratefully of the success of the ragged tail with its faded blue feathers, and patted it against his shirt to reassure himself. He bent through the doorway of the schoolroom, noting the nervous strained faces of his friends as they sat upright at their wooden desks. The blank sheets of paper before them, and Mr Hobbs pacing the aisles and impatiently consulting his watch, heightened the tension of the examination atmosphere.

'Oh, ho – what's that you've got there?' Mr Hobbs's voice boomed . characteristically through the room, and Onyango, horrified, had glanced at the suspicious bulge in his shirt, from which protruded a tiny blue feather.

'You know perfectly well that nothing is allowed to be brought into the examination-room!' And with a quick movement, the master had withdrawn the precious charm. The class had laughed, and their hoots of derision had made Onyango even more conscious of the red flush searing his neck. How could they understand? Mr Hobbs had made some very caustic comments on schoolboy superstition, and the boys revelled in Onyango's discomfiture as the sacred talisman was dropped with a sacrilegious gesture on the master's desk. Onyango knew that he had acquitted himself badly as he scribbled in the fury of humiliation, and afterwards, avoiding the excited clusters of his classmates, he had run with stumbling steps to his father's farm there to bury his head in his pillow, and weep unashamedly and uncontrollably in an impotent rage.

He had made his decision that evening: nothing mattered now – school, home, examinations: the talisman was gone, and nothing was left except his blind hate of the ogre schoolmaster. Memories of the classroom, loud with scornful laughter, only served to strengthen his resolve, and he had slipped out quietly in the damp dawn, clutching his bundle. Only in the Big City could he lose himself and his memories of that bitter morning. A feeling akin to triumph, mixed with fear of the enormity of his decision, pervaded him as he trudged townwards, kicking up little spurts of red dust with his bare toes. He pulled a banana from his bundle and bit at it savagely.

The big man in the corner was watching him covertly. Onyango sensed his curiosity, and pushed his cloth bundle closer under the table with his blistered feet. So this was the City. Once, when he was very young, his father had taken him to hospital here, but he remembered nothing except the dingy

squalor of the close-packed houses and the stinking alleyways.
The big man was still eyeing him with an intent stare from the
dark recess of the bar, and Onyango, avoiding those narrow
eyes, and hurriedly focusing on his glass, gulped down the brown
liquid. The drink stung his throat and left an acrid taste in his
mouth, but the road had been hot, and he was grateful for the
wetness. Only ninety cents left: he must be careful. 'You don't
look too happy, sonny.'

Onyango was only conscious of the flabby man's vast bulk, as
he eased himself into the other chair and blew a mist of pungent
smoke over the table. A limp cigarette dangled from narrow lips.
Despite the other's friendly tone, Onyango resented the intrusion
into his private melancholy, and besides, he felt ill-at-ease under
the shadow of those restless hypnotic eyes. But already the City's
scurrying crowds of featureless faces and the brooding grey
buildings had made Onyango aware of his own strangeness,
and here was the first soul to talk to him, even if the grating
voice came from a pouched face from which peered the most
humourless eyes Onyango had ever seen. In a welter of self-
pity, Onyango spilled out his story, only conscious of his own
misery. The big man just nodded sagely, occasionally inhaling
deeply at the bent cigarette, now burnt to a wet stub. His
eyes never left Onyango, and transfixed the boy with their cold
light.

'How much money have you got?'

Onyango's ninety cents fell on the table with a metallic clatter.

'Won't get far on that!'

Onyango shook his head, tight-lipped.

'How'd you like to earn a man's money?'

Onyango looked up quickly and suspiciously.

'S'easy. All you've got to do is pass a bunch of keys through a
window. Tsuma will do the rest. One hundred shillings for ten
minutes' work. Not bad, eh?'

Onyango stared at him incredulously. What was the man
talking about?

'Just this. The boys have found a place that's got some good
stuff – heavy silver, clothes. It's a cert – but we need a good slim

youngster like yourself to squeeze through the garage door. It's an easy five quids' worth. How about it?'

What he means, thought Onyango, is robbery! Never. He was not going to be caught as easily as that, even if he did only have ninety cents! He reached nervously for his bundle under the table. Those black eyes were watching every move.

'Sorry, don't mix with thieves.' Onyango straightened up and looked the big man in the face. Must get out of here quickly, he urged himself.

'And what if it was your good friend the teacher's place?'

A cold smile was playing on those thin lips, and the eyes watched Onyango's face. Onyango's thoughts whirled. No, it couldn't be true.

'You know where the keys are?'

Yes, he did. Hanging on a rack in the study where, at tutorials, he had often seen them. Suddenly a violent resurgence of hate against the man who had led him to this blinded his eyes, and he saw the vast shape before him only through a mist of vengeful tears, as he blurted hoarsely: 'O.K. When?'

'Tonight suits me – come on and meet the boys!'

They sped through the darkness, the car bumping over the rough road. Now Onyango felt sick with fear. I've never done anything like this before, he thought. But it should only be ten minutes, then I can collect the money and be off. The big man had promised. Never again. Onyango was startled by the car purring to a halt by the roadside. He peered out of the window: the sight was familiar. Yes, there was Mr Hobbs's house, silhouetted together with the eucalyptus trees against the pilot light glowing in the dark shadows. This was it.

'All set. Remember the back window should open outwards. Tsuma will be waiting. Take this.' The big man handed Onyango a short metal lever. 'Ready?'

Onyango nodded dumbly, his stomach cold and hollow.

The night wind stung his face as he crept along in the shadow of the hedge, its leaves rustling nervously in the darkness. He gripped the jemmy so tightly that his knuckles showed raw-red.

Only another fifty yards. He reached the garage door, feeling the force of his heartbeats against his chest, their rhythmical thud the only sound in the deep night. There was just enough space under the garage door, so it took him only a few minutes of intensive belly-wriggling to worm his way through the opening. He spat dust. Groping forward in darkness, he reached the study door. His fingers, clammy with perspiration, slipped on the handle as he soundlessly pushed the door ajar. The study was dimly lit by the suffused glow from the pilot light outside, casting long shadows on the book-lined shelves and the heavy desk. But there – on the desk – what was that? His heart leaped as he moistened his lips.

A bunch of blue feathers attached to a monkey tail lay on the top of a pile of papers.

No harm could come to him now!

Unbelievingly, he reached forward and grasped the talisman, and as he did so, his own name, in his own handwriting, stared up at him in the yellow light. Onyango's eyes widened incredulously as he saw the inked mark and the praising comment alongside – just before the lever dropped from his shocked fingers. The metal crashed to the floor with a deafening sound. Rigid with fear and incapable of movement, he heard Mr Hobbs's sleep-weary voice shout: 'Who's there?'

Onyango looked around in panic, and then bolted out of the study, heedless of the bangs and shouts in his headlong dash to reach the garage door. He squirmed underneath, tearing his clothes and face, leaped the hedge, and stumbled into the roadway. Suddenly, without warning, he was caught in the powerful headlights, bearing down on him like two gigantic suns burning the night. He felt the shock of an immense weight and heard the scream of squealing brakes. Then blackness.

Later another car door banged. A shape bent over the crumpled and inert body. Then Onyango's father saw, in the tight-clutched bleeding hand, a broken blue feather.

M. Karienye

WHERE THE WIND BLOWS

'It had been a life of struggles'

It was after midnight and Muigai – Peter Muigai – fatigued with the day's herding, had just got between two warm cow hides, the only bedding on his rugged raft of a bed.

Smoke was settling down into a milky canopy above the floor of his hut, a round windowless ramshackle which he shared with no one but a handful of sheep. Dying embers glowed dimly, almost undecidedly, at the centre of the circular mud floor; and Muigai turned. He turned again. He kept turning. It was stuffy and smoky inside the hut and he could not fall asleep no matter how much he tried!

Why could he not sleep? After all, had he not said prayers to the God of his tribe – Murungu – for his own and his sheep's safe keeping over the night? In the end had he not said another prayer to the God of the white man? There must be a reason why he could not sleep. There is a cause for everything that happens. So he worried himself for hours, every doubt leading to the next.

Muigai was one of the three baptized elders in Gituamba village. The effect of the white man's religion was just making headway in this part of Gikuyu land. Muigai and a few others had often gathered round the white man in his white robes as he talked with his black book in his hand. They had been told about a *new* God – the God who did not eat meat. The white man had claimed Mugai and the others for his strange God.

As far as Muigai was concerned, it did not matter what the white man and his mouthpiece said. What did matter was the white calico sheets he got in the way of salary for his attendance. The brown sugar, the beads and the new name, Peter, tipped the balance in favour of his attending the white man's spectacular lectures on a strange God instead of going to a beer party with Kiarie, Kiragu and the other elders of his age group. His fellows had often rebuked him for indulging in the white man's 'pack of nonsense'. 'After all, what is it that the God of the Agikuyu could not provide? He has sent rain to the people every season: he has never failed them in any way. Your once immense flock of sheep is fast dwindling away because you are torn between two Gods. The God of your ancestors can't put up with that. Your forefathers can't bear it . . .' they would always conclude.

These things flashed through Muigai's mind like an un-controlled film-reel unwinding itself. He could not sleep, he con-cluded, because something was the matter with his life. It had been a life of struggles. He had sought for rest from this and then from that. He had tried the ancestral magic, and now he had more or less fallen back on a strange deity – a deity who, for all he knew, might have been in competition with his traditional Murungu.

His two wives had perished with the last season's drought. His children had suffered under it and now his sheep were on the verge of disappearance. He himself was fast growing thin; although he was a number of seasons younger than his neighbour Kamau, the village women were constantly gossiping about his seeming the elder of the two. Could there be some truth in it all? Could it really be true that the God and the ancestors of his people had turned away from him while he groped for a strange deity? He felt frightened, afraid – afraid of something he did not understand very clearly. Somehow in his fright he fell into some sort of trance and he saw a struggle, a bitter conflict between Murungu and his ancestors on the one hand, and the God of the white man on the other. It was as if he was being pulled from two ends – the way a string is pulled to make a bow. Tension mounted. He gave vent to a dismal cry – and the cock crew. It

was its third crowing but somehow he had not heard the first
two. The crowing of the cock, however, meant that sunrise was
not many hours away. Something had to be done before sunrise.
He had to make peace with Murungu and his ancestors.

Alone in the maddening silence, therefore, he fell back to
prayers to the God of his people. His heart was heavy. He wept
bitterly in repentance and promised Murungu a goat without
blemish. 'As soon as it is day,' he prayed, 'I will make my way to
where the wind blows. On the hill, under the Mugumo-tree I'll
say prayers to you, oh Murungu of my people. I'll do it as my
forefathers used to do. I'll offer you a sacrifice as they did. I am
sure you will not fail me for you never failed them.' And with an
energetic '*Thai, thaa thaiya Ngai, thaai*' ('May it be so'), he con-
cluded his last prayer. Now there was peace in his heart and he
fell asleep just before dawn.

Sunrise at Gituamba is usually beautiful but it was exceptionally beautiful when Muigai woke up that morning. There was a
gentle leisurely atmosphere. Behind the distant Kirinyaga,
Mount Kenya, the sun was rising slowly and the light stole
gradually into the idle valleys of Gituamba.

Muigai watched the valley bottoms and the racing rays of the
sun with admiration. At the upper side of one of the valleys, a hill
rose. Muigai knew that from time immemorial his people had
climbed up that hill and offered sacrifices to Murungu. He knew
that before long he would be there – under the great Mugumo-
tree; roasting meat and uttering incantation.

All this time, however, weighty considerations occupied his
mind. Was he sure that he had broken all ties with the God of the
white man? What about this new name – this 'Peter' business?
He wondered whether he was really ready to dispense with the
sugar and the calico sheets as he started off for the Hill of the
Wind, his white goat on his broad shoulders.

The path leading to the sacred hill had not been used for a long
time now and it was overgrown with grass and bushes. It could,
however, just be traced. It took him down a valley, across a
river and up the edge of a forest. The lower reaches of the Hill

of the Wind were wooded although the top was as bare as a play-
ground. A large Mugumo-tree, however, stood at the hill's peak,
thus breaking the monotonous emptiness. Muigai panted and
sighed, his live load struggling on his shoulders. He was unhappy
and he still felt that someone else and not himself was advancing
towards the foot of the sacred tree. He was still conscious of his
inner conflict, and the nearer he got to the tree, the greater the
strain became. Yet he had made a promise to the God of the
Agikuyu which had to be fulfilled.

At last he was there, at the top of the Hill of the Wind, under
the sacred tree. Here a fierce breeze blew week-long. It was
among the yelling Mugumo leaves in this wind that the God of
the Agikuyu met his people.

Muigai made ready for the ceremony. It was to be performed
with great care. It was to be short, as the ancestors who were also
to be consulted had maintained that such ceremonies should be
performed early in the morning. The goat was to be strangled,
not killed in the ordinary way. Its blood was to be collected and
preserved. He did everything according to tradition.

The following day was Sunday. Early in the morning the bells
of the village chapel could be heard ringing in the mist. As usual,
the white man was going to preach to the villagers and among
others he would expect to find Muigai in the chapel. On the
previous day, however, Muigai had committed himself to the
God of his people. Was he to go to the chapel or was he not?
Had he not promised Murungu that he would never meddle with
the God of the white man again? How about the sugar and the
calico sheets? Could he really afford to part with them? He had
to make a decision and make it quickly, as the first song was
already in progress.

He could find a compromise, he thought. He would attend the
service but he would avoid taking it seriously. After all, there
was the sugar and the cloth. Surely the attendance would be in
his own best interest. Having reached this conclusion, he hurried
to the squalid village chapel. As usual everybody was seated and
the white man read from his Black Book. What he read was

characterized by 'Thou shalt not's'; at the end of a series of these
came 'Thou shalt not have any other God'. Muigai was struck
with a pang of guilt. Deep down in his heart he knew, he was
sure, he had 'another god' – the God of his tribe who dwelt
where the wind blew.

The service went on and on and every phrase uttered seemed
to point at him. He – a follower of two deities – was assured
eternal damnation. He contemplated confessing to the white
man that he was lost; that he did not belong anywhere. He
approached the white man but somehow the words stuck in his
throat.

That evening Muigai went to bed exceptionally early. If he
slept at all that night, it was only to imagine his insides being
gnawed by his ancestors. A ghostly creature calling out through
a speaking trumpet summoned him to the Hill of the Wind. His
mind turned desperately from the Hill of the Wind to the white
man's service until, in wild terror, he promised his deceased kin
that at the first streak of dawn he would be there – on the Hill of
the Wind, under the hissing Mugumo leaves. Now he did not
care which God he cherished. He would make it a full-scale
competition between the God of the Agikuyu and the white
man's God. Whichever increased his flock and brought pros-
perity to his home would be the winner. Was there a better way
of judging the two Gods?

On one occasion Muigai was exceptionally late on the sacred
hill. He watched the light steal away as darkness gradually took
its place on the earth. Curls of the sacred smoke rose high – high
up into the dark firmament. He felt proud, proud because he
was doing what he ought to have always done.

It was all quiet – as quiet as a graveyard. Only the ceaseless
wind faintly disturbed the leaves above the scene when, suddenly,
there was a rustling of the fallen dry leaves. Someone was
approaching the bottom of the tree. Muigai started. Could it be
his ancestors? He would not dare set eyes on them. Fear oozed
out of him as he hastily climbed up the tree. It was then that he
watched the truth unwind itself.

For countless generations his people had believed it was their God and the ancestors who devoured their sacrificial meat. And what did he see? Less than twenty feet below him a flock of fat hyenas fought over the flesh. So after all it was these beasts and not Murungu nor the ancestors that had fed on the tribe's goats without blemish for ages past. It was small wonder then that they were so fat. Muigai was bewildered at the sight. His people had been cheated – misused rather – too long.

The Hill of the Wind was not worth the reverence it had always had since Gikuyu and Mumbi, his wife, brought forth the tribe. It could not solve his problems. It could not give him peace. It was void of satisfaction – the satisfaction he had always sought. The Hill of the Wind and all it entailed was, therefore, a failure.

What about the white man's religion? It had equally failed. All it did, he complained angrily, was to issue too many threats. It was no good! He had rather have ready property and not 'the kingdom to come'. But the brown sugar and the calico sheets were worth consideration.

Tilak Banerjee

POEM

Turkishbath afternoon
   and cool tinkles of jazz
lazy contemplation
   of lazy lizards on dappled walls
icebergs and iced drink on my mind
   and throbbing sleepless
      here I recline

Novel covers stare
diary awaits cynic air
heart beats voodoo drums
life becomes humdrum
sweat on eyelids
every muscle a snail
I taste my nails
wait

she said she'd come
I'll make her serve me lime.

AN ORISSAN LOVE STORY

I met a blind man today. He was born with dark seeing eyes and he saw the sky and the sea and men. He rode the wicked and beautiful sea: his youth was exuberant. Then one day half of him died on the sand, and the moon and all the world burnt black into darkness. And the darkness still lives. It will live while he lives.

This is the story of his blindness. He sat on the shore and he said:

'The sand has begun to cool now. I can tell you the colour of the sky and the colour of the sea – and the beach. I can tell you of the gulls and the hawks, how they scream in hovering circles above the netted fish. I can exactly describe the temple of Jagannath gleaming like a mirage on the sea. And I can tell you of the men huddling around the boats with their women and their children . . . Oh, I can see them all with the great weeping eye of my mind.

'The sand is an eye which blazes in the sun and glimmers beneath the moon. The sky has eyes, millions. The sea is an eye. The birds, the fish, the Temple, the boats have eyes – the men have eyes. Eyes, eyes, eyes; but mine taken from me . . . Many eyes saw what happened to me that night of the full moon so many years ago. Look about you, stranger, while you have eyes, and live. Has not the sand gone sheet-pale; the sky become pink? Soon it will turn to violet and deepen away into pitch-blackness . . . Then half the world will be in darkness and men will light their lanterns and say their prayers, faces in the lamp-light; and the lovers grateful to the darkness will embrace in quiet ecstasy.

'Listen to the gulls and hawks crying wildly about the boats at the thrashing fish. You will find feathers on the sand . . . and naked children . . . The Temple of Jagannath like the God himself stands stoic above the swelling sea. You can hear the wind, the breakers. The foam is dead white and the deep blue of the water is greying with the approach of night. The men are like clay

gods – beautiful! Perhaps I too am beautiful? Perhaps the girls
look at me – with a bold frankness because I am blind and cannot
stare back and make them blush. There is a girl who even loves
me, seeing me blind but proud. Her voice is sweet and lovely and
she is beautiful. Oh, the flute-like music of her voice! At least, at
least I can hear . . . and I can touch and taste and smell . . . If I
dared to, if she let me embrace her, I know her head would stop
at my breast; she is so little. I know . . . One day I will let
her lead me to a bed in the warm, wet sand which the runaway
tide leaves. I shall touch her tenderly with my fingers and my
lips.

'But the story, stranger. If you were here on the beach at dawn
in the hush before the gulls, you would know the bleak splendour
of early morning, with the sea the only live thing before you,
pawing and snarling like a sullen beast, eyeing you warily as you
approached her pushing your spear-like canoe across the sand.
You would plough through a thrashing sea in the grey light and
make for the River Chilka rowing frenziedly, fighting against
the hostile waves and cold. You would have to ride two vast
breakers before you reach the calms. And then, spent, you would
rest your oars and drift. Chilka, with her swift abundance of fish,
would welcome you to her brown breast. Oh, what a joy it is to
cast your net; to flare it out and see the golden splash . . . to drag
it in for the silver catch.

'I shall never again be carried on the wings of water; never
again exult in my strength at the oar, in my skill with the net . . .
Never see again the mocking sea, the fish, the sunset, the men . . .

'We had come back that fateful day with a wonderful catch.
For a whole week or more before that we had caught little else
than pathetic little streaks of mackerel and hilsa, barely spawned.
We sacrificed to the God Jagannath then, on the night before the catch, yielding up several goats to Him and dancing
around the sacrificial fires with burning incense in our hands.
Our spirits were possessed that night and we were wild as the
drum beat . . .

'None of us slept. We whispered the darkness feverishly away.
Some went seeking their sweethearts. Sunita was only a child

then and whenever she looked at me with child-love in her great dark eyes I would stare arrogantly back. Blushing and confused, she would hurry away while I smiled scornfully at her little figure in fluttering escape. Very beautiful she was, but only a slender girl . . . She must be a goddess now, full and ripe, her dancer's gait and rich sweet voice making every man throb with desire for her . . . lovely, lovely woman now. That night, somehow, I thought of her for the first time as a lover, and smiled tenderly as her beauty filled my mind like wine. I smiled and the tenseness went out of me, and there was peace.

'We ran out on the cold, white sand to greet the dawn. We rowed to Chilka confident that Jagannath would not fail us. We murmured His name and rowed with a great eagerness . . . Evening came and we were back across the breakers. The sky dripped crimson and the sun fell into the sea like a drop of blood. All the fish-folk were gathered on the beach, tense and pallid for the catch. There was joy that evening and we sang hymns to Jagannath in vast chorus.

'What a feast we had, what dancing, what singing. The women, savage in their rhythm, danced, danced. She was not among them but sat away from us in the shade of a drooping palm, stealing glances at me from time to time, and I at her. The beach was speckled with lovers as it had been heaped with fish. But we, Sunita and I, had to be content with shy gazing and, at last, a few shy words . . . Only, the men drank too much toddy at the feast and there was a fight.

We were studying one another mutely in the soft light of dusk. Then suddenly, a voice broke out, agonized as a dying bird's. I heard a scream from a little hut, my dear mother's cry. I ran across and into her dwelling, with horror in my breast. My mother . . . lay on the floor . . . sari torn . . . eyes closed in shame and pain, semi-conscious, a man like some demon, standing over her. Wizened and old he was, but agile as a panther. Even in his drunkenness, he was quick and strong and cunning. In one flash he had left her, leapt up, thrown me aside and vanished into the night. But the moon was full and bright: I would find him, and I had recognized him. Gopal! But Mother, what of you? I raised her, covered her with a sheet, laid her on the bed. Quickly I built a fire in the hut and forced water down her throat. She stirred and moaned. Her tiny white hands crept shuddering from under the sheet; came together. She prayed in that half-conscious, half-dead state. She prayed, her bloodless lips moving, her eyes pinched. Was she going to die? But suddenly it seemed as though she were drifting off into sleep in her shock. I left her and closed the door gently behind me. Did I hear her softly call my name as I ran? I think she had called me. I should have come back to see. But I didn't: I looked at the moon, the great silver, beautiful moon, and I ran, cursing, cursing, cursing through the huge, howling wind . . I knew he must have fled to the boats to hide. A terrible intuition told me. So I ran, crying terribly for vengeance. I had a knife.

'I came to the boats and shrieked his name. Gopal he was called. The Lord Krishna was called Gopal in adoration for the sweet innocence he displayed in his youth. No god, this Gopal, but a devil: he did not love, he; he raped, he ravished widows, and left them dying.

'I saw him. He had a great oar in his hands as he rose from behind a boat, the moon shining grotesquely on his leering face . . . What devil gave him the strength to swing that oar? I ducked and dived, I buried my six inches of steel between his loins and saw him die. I laughed him to his death. It was I the devil then.

'How Gopal's friends happened to come suddenly upon me I do not know. I never knew who brought me to the gates of Yama's Kingdom. But a blow came, and another, and another: blows across my skull and across my eyes; a fierce, burning darkness descended and I collapsed. I must have screamed and saved myself from death. Because I went home alive in a litter. They carried me to the old herbalist. When I came to, I discovered I was blind. Blind. Like a frightened child I cried out for my mother.

'Then I heard Sunita's voice and felt her cold fingers on my chest. "*Arjun, Arjun*", she sobbed. "Your mother – she is dying"; and she fell on my neck weeping. I was numb. Then I cried, "Take me to my mother." Silently, with the reverence that men

give only to their saints, I was borne to the hut. I would not let
my mother know that she was leaving behind her a sightless son.
So I ordered them to stop before the little shack. I felt my way:
and I knew where to kneel. "Mother, Mother, why are you
leaving me?"

'Then suddenly the horrid realization came to me. The acrid
smell of fire and burnt flesh and cloth hit me like a blow. I
touched my mother's brow, and charred skin came away.
"Mother," I cried, "what have you done? What have I done to
you?" And I cursed Jagannath.

'"Hush," she whispered and touched me with her hand,
"Hush, my child, you did nothing to me. I love you so much . . ."
She paused to caress my hand. She spoke again, her voice a
murmured burble of sound. "I have burned myself as a widow
should. This is my *suttee*. You are grown now . . . By now I
should have been ashes but the good villagers were cruel and
quenched the flames. Still the pain, ah, the pain . . . It is like
child-birth except the whole body is in torment now . . . But
Arjun, your mother is brave. And blaspheme not, my son. They
will not let me enter heaven if you do." Her arms came up,
uncertain, seeking. Suddenly I realized that she too was blind.
But she was dying and I would live.

'"Did he . . . did he soil you, Mother?" She must have smiled
sadly for her mouth trembled in my palm and her tears washed
it: "Yes, my child, that is why I could not live. Your father, I
hope, will greet me in the next world . . . I bless thee with long
life and happiness." She kissed my head, moaned out: "Blood,
blood here, my son, you have bled from some wound . . ." I
could not bear it and put my hand to her lips: "It is nothing,
Mother," I was able to say as I kissed her hair.

'She died, leaving me behind, blessing me with long life; not
knowing that she had really cursed me. Blind, and live a long
life! She died young like a champak blossom torn off the branch
for a savage scenting and then thrown to suddenly shrivel in the
dust.

'But perhaps there *is* hope; there is Sunita: and, stranger, is not
a maiden coming down the path, looking like a goddess and

E

treading the sand like a dancer? I hear the tinkle of her silver anklets. It must be she. Sunita, Sunita, come here, my love. Put your fish-baskets aside and come to me; I can wait no longer. Go, stranger, and leave me to my love. "Mother, will you receive her unto your household?"'

Solomon Kagwe

TO A FARM IN THE WHITE HIGHLANDS

The basic economy of Kenya depends on agriculture in the White Highlands. Nearly all commodities for export, such as maize, coffee, pyrethrum and wheat are grown in this area. The best butter in East Africa also comes from the White Highlands. There is no doubt, therefore, that the farms in the settled area command a wide interest not only from those people whose homes are in Kenya but also from those in foreign countries. It would be useful and interesting for you to visit a typical farm belonging to Mr Brown, where I was born and brought up and which I visit regularly to see my relatives. But before you go there, it is important, if you are an African, that you change any smart clothes you may have and put on dirty ones. If they are ragged, the better. You may resent this but there is no alternative. Mr Brown knows the educated people by the way they dress and does not allow these people 'from the town' to visit his farm. He says that they suffer from chronic infectious laziness and that they have strange ideas which his workers do not desire.

When you look around his big farm, you start wondering where his workers live. All you see are small mud-and-wattle huts huddled together and perhaps you may think that these are stables. You would be mistaken, for these are workers' houses. A barbed-wire fence and a big trench surround these huts. Mr Brown has told the workers that this is necessary to keep thieves away. Opposite this village, as these huddled huts are usually called, is Mr Brown's house which is a quarter of a mile away. But it has no fence around it.

The farm, which covers about a thousand acres, has many good and fat cows, sheep and pigs. Some other parts of the farm are devoted to coffee, pyrethrum and tea.

When you go there, you meet bare-footed people who are thin and hungry-looking. They are all invariably in soiled and tattered clothes. Let them learn that you come from the town and that you have a little education. At first they will be surprised at your ragged clothes. They always expect a person from the town to be in a suit. They will then show you their hospitality. You will be led to one of their huts. On seeing the inside of the hut you cannot help being moved to pity and sympathy. At the same time, you will be astonished to learn that some human beings can live in conditions which you never dreamt of. The hut is their kitchen, dining-room, bedroom, bathroom. All members of the family sleep there. In a typical hut, you will see a bed for the mother and another one for the father. All children sleep on the bare floor together with fleas and sheep. But these people appear happy. The boys sing and play during the day and the evening time. You would never think that they will go to sleep on the floor where about four of them will share one blanket. They do not go to school for there is not one. Mr Brown thinks that these boys should grow up to replace their parents when they retire from working for him. In his belief that education makes a person lazy, he has resisted all attempts by his workers to build a Village School. The workers will tell you how they like meeting people from the towns. You will have noticed this long before they say it. They welcome you to their houses smiling, and give you the best stool in the hut, specially for visitors. The mother of the hut will busy herself preparing porridge while the children stand gazing at you admiringly. The neighbours of your host come to greet you and express pleasure at your visiting them. Their appearance, their smiling faces and their pleasant gestures will make you think they are happy; but in this village during a working day you will wonder whether some people do not need hell's fire to make them look unhappy.

They wake up at 4.30 a.m. They prepare themselves for work. The mothers cook for their children and then all go to the farm at about 6 a.m. leaving their young ones behind. No sooner do they reach their places of work than they meet Mr Brown and his overseers. Watch these people clearing and digging a new area for plantation and you see what a mighty job they have to do. The women clear the bush. The men follow them, digging, while the young boys break the large lumps of soil. As soon as a boy is over five years old he goes to do this job. Mr Brown says that this is the best age for offering young boys the earliest opportunity of apprenticeship to the job they hope to do, that of digging and harvesting his crops.

All the workers do their job without rest – not because they do not know the dangers of overwork but because the prospects of being seen standing idle are not pleasant. A slight pause is enough to make the angry Mr Brown decide not to give a person his day's wages. In the absence of Mr Brown, his wife takes over. She is not the sort of person either who would get tired of watching the workers. Go near where they work. The earth shakes under men's heavy hoes. They do this job without break up to 8 p.m. in the evening, with only fifteen minutes at 12 o'clock when they can snatch their lunch. This consists of porridge and one or two sweet potatoes. You wonder whether this is sufficient when you consider the amount of work they have to do but Mr Brown will tell you that a person who eats much grows lazy and that is why he gives them fifteen shillings a month. After 12.15 p.m., all, including children, resume their work, now in the blazing afternoon sun. Men and boys remove their shirts. The former continue breaking the ground as before. You can see swift streams of sweat running down their slender bodies. Their faces become wet with perspiration. Often they use their torn handkerchiefs to dry themselves. But they do not spend a minute to do this. The Browns or their obsequious overseers are quick at seeing 'lazy' people.

While working, these people keep away tedium by singing as

soldiers do in order to elevate their spirits and courage. It is
interesting to notice a verse of one of these songs which runs as
follows:

> Since you erred, Adam,
> We've got to sweat
> And like tractors work
> For all our lives
> To earn our living.

Mr Brown knows that his workers are simple and religious
people who are not aware that they have rights. That is why he
works them from 6 a.m. to 8 p.m.

After work at 8 p.m. the people wearily plod their way home-
wards. The mothers start the tiring business of cooking while
the hard-worked men relax on their hard stools. The mothers
first of all cook light food for their hungry, crying children, who
have not been with their parents all the day long. They cry
because they have not had enough food during the day. If you
have been to a cattle *boma* (a Swahili word for a cattle dwelling)
and have heard the clamour that calves make in the evening while
waiting for their mothers, then you know what to expect in this
village.

After they have had their supper, the tired workers go to bed
and then start their dreary routine at 4.30 a.m. the following
morning.

N. G. Ngulukulu

A PRESCRIPTION

It was not a time of dearth. Far from it. Corn had been harvested and stored in granaries, and these had been filled to the brim. Meat too was plentiful as also were beans and potatoes. But Mr Doggrel could find no satisfaction in such nourishment, though it is true he ate his fill when meals of this kind were put before him.

'Still,' as he told his wife on one occasion, 'I get the feeling that I have not absorbed the proper ingredients. What the nature of those proper ingredients might be, I really don't know. I can only guess. But don't let this bother you, my dear. Still less you, Tapo.'

This last remark was addressed to his son who was sitting opposite him in the parlour. After observing his father brighten up a little, Tapo suffered himself to undergo the same process, and then his mother said, addressing the father:

'My dear, you had better be satisfied with what you have. The attempt to gratify every desire adequately has frustrated many people more capable, richer and more imaginative than yourself. There will never be an end to your desires or to any other man's, I assure you.'

'What I really think I need,' said Doggrel, encouraged by the sympathetic disposition of his wife, 'is . . . how shall I put it? I want to say that I need the meat of – eh – any one of those creatures that bark, you know, howl, whine and all that.' He paused and then went on, 'Yes, my dear, now that I come to think of it, I am sure that is precisely what I require.'

His eyes were averted from those of his wife, who stood facing him. Mrs Doggrel, for her part, was beginning to show signs of disgust at the sheer brazenness with which her husband declared his partiality for the meat of the barking species.

'Doggrel, are you telling me that you want to eat a dog?' she queried in a manner which left her husband in no doubt as to her own attitude to such a suggestion.

'Not exactly, my dear,' he replied, casting a furtive glance at her and then reclining on the couch. 'What I mean to say is that we should capture one of these animals, cook it and then, you know, decide what to do with it.'

He laughed slightly under the impression of having explained what he meant with sufficient subtlety to make it difficult, if not impossible, for his wife to guess what he was driving at, and on the strength of this conviction he sat bolt upright and made bold to look at her. A faint smile still lingered on his face; but it disappeared as soon as he noted the change in his spouse and was simultaneously succeeded by a distinct expression of a very different mood, a certain state of being which disposed him to whistle and play with his feet as though he was in a dancing hall treading a measure, but in a sitting posture.

His wife was disgusted. The idea of anybody eating a dog was so revolting to her that her first impulse was to rebuke Mr Doggrel. But then she thought perhaps her husband was only joking after all, even though she had never known him crack jokes before.

'I'll tell you what, Doggrel,' she declared, interrupting his dancing and whistling. 'If you really love me, never so much as mention this to me again. I promise you'll regret it if you do.'

Mrs Doggrel retreated to an adjoining chamber after her outburst of anger, closely followed by Tapo who was thoroughly dejected. Left to himself, Doggrel resumed his whistling and gradually lapsed into a melancholy mood. He thought of the past, of the many children who had been born to him and who had died soon after reaching the age of five or six months. Tapo was his only remaining child. Mr Doggrel wanted to have more. The regularity with which his children had died off had led

Doggrel to suspect that his house was under the influence of some malicious being. Whether that being was human or divine he could not tell. Nevertheless he was inclined to suspect some of his fellow human beings since he thought he knew these better than those which he had never seen. The outcome of his suspicion was that he went to see many people who, he thought, were capable of suggesting ways out of his situation. He got advice from all of them, in return for money each time. Yet although he followed their instructions with minute care, no improvement whatsoever was apparent. Children were born and died in their infancy much as if the father had not moved a finger in an attempt to enable them to live longer.

As a last resort Doggrel had decided to consult Mr Ober, who was famed for the accuracy of his prescriptions and the effectiveness of his remedies, more so than anybody else; and this he had done without the knowledge of his wife. He had gone to see the famous man at night to avoid being noticed by his friends and neighbours; and Mr Ober had been so obliging as to let him observe how, from such a premise as the frequent deaths of Doggrel's children, he arrived at the conclusion which determined the prescription Doggrel was eventually given.

It was a serious business. Indeed at one stage in the process Doggrel almost ran out of the laboratory in spite of himself. For Mr Ober, having suitably arrayed himself in ceremonial robes and having equipped himself with the tail of a cow, a bundle of sticks and an earthen pot, was performing the ritual in a frantic manner. His body was convulsed and his eyes, like tiny stars, withdrew, or seemed to do so, farther into their sockets so that Doggrel took fright. Soon the whole place was filled with sparks and the consultant lost sight of the adviser. He could only hear his voice, which jarred on his ears so that he got the illusion that he was the one who was imploring whatever powers there were for help and this multiplied his fear. He was about to run away when suddenly the air cleared and he could see his companion again. Ober immediately issued the prescription and Doggrel readily accepted it. He had no doubt it would prove effective, in view of all that had gone to the making of it, and that is why he was determined to follow it to the last detail.

'I might as well die as give up the attempt to save my children,' he declared, and went out.

Mrs Doggrel did not hear what he said. Neither did she notice his going out. She was playing with Tapo and that engaged all her attention. She was a good woman and set great store by her principles. Nothing could divert her from them, and Doggrel knew this.

Among the Doggrels' neighbours was a lady who owned a very big dog. Her name was Mrs Fedo and she was so much attached to that animal that she would not suffer anybody to throw so much as an unkind word to it. She had broken many tender and long-standing friendships when they were found to be incompatible with her devotion to this favourite. One morning the whole village was thrown into great confusion by the announcement that Mrs Fedo's dog had been stolen! The thief, it was said, was of an unusual type. He took away the dog and substituted for it a dummy which looked so much like the original that Mrs Fedo had initially mistaken it for her own. She had then called it by its name and, getting no response, she had suspected the dog of developing stubbornness as a challenge to her in her old age. This had infuriated her so much that she had forthwith taken a stick and lashed the object of her fury till she was dog-tired. The inability of the dummy to howl was taken by the vexed woman as evidence of the dog's complete change of heart and so it provoked her anger all the more. That she was wasting her corrective efforts did not occur to her until she was completely exhausted and then it was only to throw her into a state of coma which was subsequently described by the doctor as 'rather serious'.

At first the neighbours were deeply concerned about it all, and some even went in quest of the missing pet. But when they fell to examining her attitude towards the dog, most of them, instead of grieving, rejoiced that it was missing.

'This will probably readjust her emotional and mental attitude to the world,' said one man sipping wine in a bar. 'If it does that,

whoever deprived her of the dog deserves the name of phil-
anthropist,' observed Doggrel, fortifying himself with a quantity
of beer. 'That dog absorbed the whole of her attention. It was
even rumoured she intended to bequeath her money to it when
she died!'

'Just think of that!' remarked the other. 'I'm sure I don't regret
she's been deprived of it. Maybe she will dispose of her property
more prudently. The dog may have been snatched by a hyena or
some such wild animal. I don't think anybody would ever dream
of taking it for himself, do you?'

Doggrel said he did not think so either and drank his beer. It
was obvious that he was not interested in speculation, and so his
companion abandoned himself to the pleasurable business of
becoming a 'blessed being' through the effects of wine.

'I want to know exactly what happens when wine is added to
personality, that is, if I may express it mathematically, the product of "personality + alcohol". You are not going to tell me
the thing is too abstract, Doggrel, are you?' he said and then
burst into laughter. Doggrel was not interested. He drank his
beer in silence. Even when his delighted companion became so
excited about the mathematical formula as to overbalance himself
and fall from his high stool, Doggrel remained unmoved.

After six months had elapsed another villager lost her dog.
Of an evening this lady would take a stroll in canine company
along a certain path that led to a well. She was so much in the
habit of using that path that she would use no other if her intention was to take the air. On the occasion when her dog and she
were to part for ever, she was reading a pamphlet on *The Psycho-
logy of Domestic Pets,* and the dog was lagging behind. Suddenly
she heard a noise somewhat similar to that often made by her
dog and turning round just in time she saw what she thought was
her pet skip lightly and fall headlong into a tiny thicket.

'Come on!' she called, but got no reply.

'Come on, Maggie!' she entreated, but still there was no
response.

'Now if I come there, I'll give it to you, Maggie, I assure you.'
No answer came even then.

'Maggie!' she cried, beginning to lose her patience. When this too was followed by silence, she clicked her tongue and retraced her steps in great resentment.

'Why don't you come when I call, you stupid pup – Oh!' She was hurt. She could scarcely believe she was awake. For what she had in her arms was not Maggie but an imitation spaniel with an elaborate clockwork motor inside which made it jump about when the spring was wound up. She cast her eyes everywhere for the real Maggie. It was to be seen nowhere.

'This is the work of Mrs Fedo!' she said at last. 'I'll find out what she means by it,' and away she went to seek information. She was so indignant that she ran the whole distance. She could not even wait till she was in the house but exploded at the entrance.

'Mrs Fedo, what do you mean by foisting such rubbish upon me?' The other had scarcely recovered from the shock occasioned by the disappearance of her own darling, so the lady's display of an imitation dog merely served to revive the consciousness of her loss. She said nothing.

'Well, I want my puppy back within half an hour. If you do not produce it, you'll find out who you're dealing with'; and, dashing the forgery on the floor, to the consternation of Mrs Fedo, she scurried away. Arriving home, she shed copious tears and was quite disconsolate. In an attempt to find out the cause of her grief, her husband went to see Mrs Fedo and was told what his wife had done there. The grieved lady denied that she had anything to do with the loss of her neighbour's puppy, and disowned the dummy which the lady had left.

'*This* is the one which I was given in the place of my beloved Phito,' she said, full of emotion, showing the toy she had been bequeathed to the inquiring husband.

'I am sure there is some mischievous person who is doing this kind of dirty business,' he declared. 'I'll ferret him out. Goodbye.'

Two more dogs were lost in the course of the following year. Then the whole thing stopped. The villagers, however, were disturbed in another way. Just before the last two pets were sundered from their owners, the sad news of the separation of Mr and Mrs Doggrel became known and this caused much talk and speculation, the more so as no adequate reason was given for it, and the couple had been known to be very much devoted to each other in spite, or possibly because of, the frequent deaths of their children. Mr Doggrel had remained in his house and his wife had gone back to her parents, together with Tapo. Doggrel had subsequently become a votary of alcoholic drinks and had been observed to take beer in such great quantities that he seemed as if he was competing with a genie whose craving for strong drink was twice as keen as his own. There were many among his neighbours and compotators who had it that '*in vino veritas*'. But they never got anything about the separation from Doggrel after he was drunk, however hard they tried to elicit information. One night, after a drinking bout, he invited a number of his friends to his house and, the invitation having been accepted, he conducted them there and gave them food to eat. He presented it on a big circular plate. The meat was in a spacious bowl. What each one of the guests had to do to allay his hunger was merely to take part of the solid stuff from the plate, roll it into a ball, press the thumb into it to make a small hole, dip it in the sauce and convey the mixture into his mouth. The process could be repeated a hundred and one times. When he felt like it, he helped himself to the meat. On this occasion the guests were extremely hilarious and all of them soon forsook what was on his plate and concentrated their interest on the more palatable contents of the bowl. They ate with zest and talked with gaiety. Said one of them: 'I keep forgetting that Doggrel is now a bachelor, having "put away his wife" as it is written in the Bible, for personal reasons.' 'To be sure,' mused another, 'Mrs Doggrel is not here. Oh, how I miss her!' and forthwith he began to weep.

'Gentlemen,' mumbled the host, who was in a state midway between sleep and waking, 'quite frankly I won't allow any one of you to poke his nose into my affairs. These are exclusively private matters. You are here to feed, remember that, not to speculate on what may have happened between my wife and myself.'

'But if the lady of the house is absent,' said the guest who was weeping, wiping his tears, 'who else can cook meat so well?'

'The husband, sir,' replied his companion. 'You should not forget that Mr Doggrel can cook as well as any domestic scientist. It is this unusual ability which, in my opinion, accounts for the separation. "Too many cooks", as the sages say, "must spoil the broth".'

'That is perfectly true,' chimed the other. 'I think you've hit on the explanation.'

'My friends,' said another guest deliberately, 'we have been eating a dog!'

'No!' chorused the others anxiously.

'Look at that.' He pointed at a sizeable piece of bone which he had been contemplating for some time. He had taken it from the bowl intent upon finally doing justice to Doggrel's hospitality, but its curious shape had made him pause and look at it more closely. He had put it on his plate and while his friends had been trying to coax their host into telling them why the hostess was not with them, he had been examining it from various angles, now using his sun-glasses and now his naked eye. At last he had arrived at the conclusion that Doggrel had given them a rare meal.

'I am sure that is a dog's snout,' said the maudlin guest. 'And to think that Doggrel could accord us such treatment! What have we done to deserve it?'

'Doggrel,' pleaded another, 'how could you behave so to us? A dog,' he said appealing to the rest of the company, 'is not only obnoxious to me. It is a taboo. I'll suffer terribly for it, and all on account of you! Let us go, gentlemen. Yet let me assure you, Doggrel, you will have to answer for this,' and having said so he left the room. The others soon followed him, shaking their heads, while Doggrel feebly denied that he had given them dog-meat to feed on.

'I am dashed if that is what anybody would – reasonably, now, eh – reasonably call the meat of a dog. What evidence is there to show that this is a dog?' he asked, examining the piece of bone. 'It is plain crooked thinking: taking the part for the whole. It's silly.'

Four days later he was summoned to court on charges of killing the dogs of his neighbours and of feeding his guests on tabooed meat. However, Doggrel no longer remembered that he had entertained guests in his house, and so he denied the charges. But when the magistrate threatened to search his house, and his wife explained to the court the reason for her separating from him two years ago, Doggrel admitted the charges.

'It was Mr Ober who told me that I could prevent the death of my children by feeding on the meat of dogs. I simply followed his instructions. I had no intention of giving the meat to my guests. I did so purely by accident.'

The confession induced laughter among the people who had assembled to hear the case. Then the magistrate said, 'It is surprising that a man who claims to be enlightened like you could believe such things. You will have to pay a fine of two hundred shillings or else go to jail for four weeks.' Doggrel chose to pay the fine.

He went home with his wife, after promising he would never eat dogs again.

'I never thought you would take it so seriously,' he said when they were seated.

'I never thought you would take it so lightly, either,' she declared, and turning her eyes away from him, she added. 'My mother forbade me utterly to eat dogs. She said I would be affected by a fatal disease the moment I did so.'

'Did she?'

'Yes.'

No more of their children died after that, because no more were born. Tapo remained the couple's only child.

Joe Mutiga

TO THE CEREMONIAL MUGUMO (FIG-TREE)

Holy huge tree, you tax my memory:
Over you boys awaiting circumcision
Proudly threw '*ndorothi*' to show ability
To shoulder social responsibility,
While all danced in heartful joy,
Bearing proudly the tribal decorum:

With proud ostrich feathers
Blowing in the dancing air,
And the rattles rattling in tune,
While all throats sang hoarse;
You are a memory of beauty,
Of annual tribal festivity;

A memory of olden days
When the Agikuyu were a tribe,
Though now but part of a nation,
A nation that is soon to be:
It is happier thus in all,
But the beauty of old is gone.

Around you was the life,
The loyalty and spirit of the tribe;
But now the ground,
On which the dancers once trod,
Is laden with the green of crops,
The holy ground no more holy;

No decorum but hoe and soil,
No dancing on the ground,
The lonely digger sweats alone;
Sweats as he destroys
The preserve of many an age;
It is sad:

Our customs are dug up
And put aside, like the grass
On which the dancer trod,
And foreign crops implanted;
And we pass by, eyes on the ground,
Submitting to the foreign as ours.

THE TEACHERS AND THE PRIEST

On his occasional rounds he walked stealthily,
Like a scout spying an enemy camp
To see where the commander lies,
And kill him first.

Through the teachers' compound, he walked;
The rosary his revolver, he roved the grounds,
Like a leopard that scents fire or man
In a hut with sheep.

The priest heard voices and stopped;
'She should be alone,' he said to himself;
He stole nearer the house and listened;
The tones were hushed.

The priest stood and listened,
Listened to the tones inside the house –
There was a bass where sure there
Shouldn't be any.

He listened but could not tell who:
The tones were hushed in fear of him;
There was no keyhole to spy through –
He had to get in.

He knocked and pushed the door;
The door resisted, he knocked again;
They had never heard his knock, but
They knew it was his.

The door was barred against intruders;
They could not bolt in, unwelcome intruders
And find her unaware, unpleasant visitors,
And confuse her.

'What is to be done? Save us Lord!'
'Who is it?' she asks. 'I, the priest.'
If 'he' is seen they are done –
No job for them.

'This teaching profession where one
Is sacked through a fool's folly.
Why not leave us alone (we are grown)
To do our will?'

Their minds worked quickly,
Their hearts bumped, not with love;
They sweat, not with mutual warmth, but
The fear of the priest.

'He' put the lamp low, knocked the table,
And there was a darkness, dark as Hell.
'This lamp is bad, touch the table it's off!'
Shouts the girl in anger.

'He' crouched and hid in her skirt;
The skirt was long, thick and wide
And hid 'him', and there 'he' sweats,
Not with her warmth.

They moved to the door, two in one,
She opened for the priest who bolted in;
Expecting to find a victim, he bolted in,
But found none.

She stood and faced him unabashed;
He stood and faced her confused;
Secretly his eyes turned under the bed
But found nothing.

The door wide open, there was light
Inside the house, but sure no man;
'Her man' squatted, the door behind him;
Stupidly gazed the priest.

The priest slowly looked around observing
As closely as a Special Branch Officer,
Or like a dog sniffing after a hunted
Animal or criminal.

She moved and stood at the door
Looking inside, shielding 'her man'.
'Will you light the candles at vespers?'
'Women never do it here.'

The priest stood in the empty room;
She stood at the door shielding 'her man';
'Her man' squatted, the night behind 'him';
And all hearts stood.

The night was cool, kind and deep;
'Her man' stirred quietly like a breeze,
And like a swamp-bird slipped off,
And the night swallowed him.

She closed the door, put on the lamp;
The room was small, the window barred;
The priest surely heard two human tones:
Where is one now?

Yes! The priest is divine, and cares for souls;
But the world must be peopled, or else no humanity,
And one can't see the flutter of a skirt,
And lead it to the altar.

Elvania Namukwaya Zirimu

THE HEN AND THE GROUNDNUTS

My mother had instructed me thoroughly in traditional cookery at an early age. By the time I was thirteen I could prepare a meal worthy to be set before any chief. It was the parish priest's habit, whenever he wanted to go round our part of the parish, to come and stay with us for a few days and go out home-visiting with my father. He was with us on one of these visits when my mother left me in charge of both preparing the evening meal and looking after the small children, as she was going to see a friend who had just had a baby.

Everything was laid out for me in the right quantities for, although good at cooking, I was liable to use either too much or too little of everything. As for groundnuts to make the sauce, my mother put out what I would need as usual, and safely locked the store to keep out the chickens and the children who, if let in, would devour any amount up to half a sack in an hour.

For some time after my mother had gone I went about my duties singing to myself and feeling very important. With the help of the little ones I shelled the groundnuts while the food steamed on the blazing wood fire. I was just telling myself that I was doing well, when I was tempted. I could hear my brothers laughing merrily as they played cards with our neighbours' children on the grass in front of our house. The game had started off mildly, and as long as it stayed that way I did not care. But it was getting more and more exciting, as the shouts and laughter demonstrated. Eventually my little sister rose up and ran out to see, if not to join in, followed by my two little brothers.

I was alone. Thoughts of self-pity overcame me. Why should the boys be playing and enjoying themselves while I alone laboured for their greedy sakes? It was not fair. Why could they not be given some of the work so that I too might have a bit of fun? I had a right to play as well as anybody else. A second wave of laughter louder than the first interrupted my thoughts. I abandoned groundnuts and all and ran out.

I could tell from the boys' stolen glances at me that I was not welcome. They could not let me come in, in the middle of a game, they said. And, as they ended in an argument as to who was the winner, I overcame my jealousy and decided to go back to my duties.

Satisfied cluckings of chickens dancing round the kitchen as they picked up the remains of a great feast reminded me of the groundnuts. Yes, every nut was gone. How stupid I had been to leave them there uncovered with the kitchen door wide open. But such self-reproach did not occur to me at the time. For I was seized by a blinding rage and an itching desire to punish the greedy, beastly offenders. Now the most annoying thing about a chicken is that you can never hit it if you intend to. You are always bound to miss it, especially if you are really cross. At your failure it will make a noise half of defiance and half of disapproval, and then march away majestically, leaving you more annoyed than ever. I added all these things up to make a sum of charges against them as I stood in the doorway, thinking how best to launch my next attack while they were still busy scratching here and there in search of a stray nut.

I seized the pestle and raised it high up above my head. By this time they had seen me and were flying in disorder all over the kitchen. They tumbled over each other through the doorway. I let down my powerful weapon just in time to hit the last one right on the head. I did hit! It was the most active hen of the lot and therefore my dearest enemy. 'Got you this time!' I gasped in triumph as it croaked painfully. But my victory song did not last, for in a minute the poor thing was staggering frantically about the kitchen. Its strength failed after a while and it fell lifeless just near the fire. I leapt to rescue it from the eager flames. I shook it, examined it, shook it again and then tried to open its closed eyes with my finger. It would not move.

I raced with it to the house, got hold of the baby's vaseline and rubbed a lump on the wound. No response. I put it down to try and make it walk but it gave a feeble 'Coo' and fell over. I applied another lump of vaseline, not that the idea of vaseline as a healing agent ever entered my head, but because it was the first thing that came my way. I carried it to a quiet part of the garden, rocking it like a baby. Seeing this had no effect I put it down and fanned it with a banana leaf.

All this time I was dreading what my father would do to me. Of course the hen was naughty and deserved punishment, I told myself. Mother would be angry with me because of the groundnuts which were to make up the sauce for supper. But then punishing the hen, let alone killing it, would not make her less angry with me. In short I was going to bring both my mother's and, worst of all, my father's anger against me by my foolish action. After five minutes' vigorous fanning without any change a thought struck me. Back to the kitchen I raced and returned with a basin of water into which I dipped the poor thing. Whether it was this unexpected happening after a long period of pretence or whether the hen had really fainted I cannot tell. But I was rewarded. Having drunk some water the hen became normal again although it showed great disgust at my conduct and especially at being wetted so ruthlessly.

'I could have sworn there were no groundnuts in that sauce last night,' said my mother the next morning. 'One could detect the tomatoes and egg plant, all right, but no groundnuts.' I held my peace.

KEEPING UP WITH THE MUKASAS

CHARACTERS

MWEBE – *a cultivator*
ZEBIA – *his wife*
NAMATA – *their daughter*
SALI – *a neighbour*
NORA – *his wife*

The play takes place in the sitting-room of Mwebe's house. The scene is the sitting-room of an upper-middle-class Muganda. The time is 1962.

SCENE ONE

Time: 11 o'clock in the morning.
Children's ironed clothes on a chair. A few toys lying on the floor.
ZEBIA is ironing on the only table in the room.
ZEBIA (*gently*): Namata. (*Pause. Without raising her voice*) Namata. (*Another wave of laughter, mingled with a child's crying.*) Namata.
NAMATA (*within*): Ye-es? (*Comes in and kneels down.*)
ZEBIA: Who was that crying?
NAMATA: Tomasi.
ZEBIA: What's the matter with him?
NAMATA: He has a banana flower which he calls his cow. When Musa came back from school he found him dragging it at the end of a string and saying it was going to eat grass, but Musa told him it was only a silly banana flower, and not a cow, so he cried.
ZEBIA: I don't see why Musa need be so provocative. You should be thinking of preparing tea now, instead of just giggling with the children. Your father will soon be back and you know what happens when he comes in from the garden and finds no tea ready. Tell Musa to get out the bicycle and

clean it. I heard your father say he would be going out this afternoon.

NAMATA: All right, Mother. (*But she does not leave the room. Instead she goes and tries to switch on the radio. She switches it off again, goes to the table and looks at some papers and magazines, one after another.*)

ZEBIA (*still gently*): Namata, go and put the kettle on. You can look at those things later.

NAMATA: Mother, why don't we have tea first thing in the morning like the Salis? They get up, eat and then do other things. They don't have to make tea at eleven o'clock. Why don't we do the same?

ZEBIA: Because it is necessary to work in the garden very early in the morning while it is still cool. The Salis don't have to work in the garden.

NAMATA: Well, let's not work in the garden, then! I'd rather eat early in the morning than go to dig.

ZEBIA: Don't be silly. Go and put the kettle on. (NAMATA *skips out.* ZEBIA *looks up at the clock. Another wave of laughter from within. She calls as gently as before.*) Namata, Namata.

NAMATA (*breathless, appearing at the door*): Yes.

ZEBIA: I told you to go and make some tea.

NAMATA: I am going, Mother. I was just telling Musa to get out the bicycle and clean it. (*Shouting*) Musa, get out father's bicycle and clean it.

ZEBIA: Don't shout.

NAMATA: Mother says so. Father is going out. (*She lingers by the entrance.*)

ZEBIA: Why don't you do what you're told?

NAMATA: What haven't I done, Mother?

ZEBIA (*a little impatiently*): I said go and make some tea. It's getting late.

NAMATA (*a little perplexed*): Eh! Shall I light the Primus or shall I make a wood fire?

ZEBIA: We cannot afford to waste paraffin when there is plenty of firewood.

NAMATA (*having disappeared, but soon coming back and lingering by the entrance*): Shall I boil the milk?

ZEBIA: Have you put the kettle on?

NAMATA (*uncertainly*): Y-yes. (ZEBIA *flashes a look at her, then lowers her eyes and resumes her work.*) Can I roast some ground-nuts, Mother? (ZEBIA *does not answer.*) Mother, shall I roast some nuts? (*No response.*) Eh — (*She goes out. More laughter within. Sudden silence. A man's voice.*)

MWEBE (*off*): Is the tea ready? (*He comes in with a parcel which he throws to his wife.*) Where is tea? (*He picks up the scattered toys one by one and throws them out.*)

ZEBIA (*putting the parcel aside*): Thank you. Please don't throw those away; the children want them.

MWEBE (*removing magazine and papers from table and throwing them on to the floor*): How many times have I told them not to leave their playthings lying around? I won't have the house turned into a banana garden. (*He tears up one of the magazines.*)

ZEBIA: Oh, please.

MWEBE (*looking up quickly*): What?

ZEBIA: If you have no more use for them, give them to the children. They like looking at the pictures.

MWEBE *impatiently continues to tear up magazines. He throws the pieces on the floor, blows away the dust from the table and then dusts it with his hand. He looks at it, pulls a face, then takes up a child's ironed garment from the chair and dusts the table vigorously with it. The noise draws* ZEBIA's *attention. She looks up and makes to speak, but shuts her mouth again and stays silent.* NAMATA *comes in with the tray which she places before her mother. She is walking on tiptoe.*

MWEBE (*pointing to the heap of torn paper*): Take them away.

ZEBIA: And when you have done that, Namata, come back and take away these clothes. That shirt will need rewashing.

NAMATA *collects up papers and tiptoes out.*

MWEBE: If no one is pouring out the tea, I'm going without it. ZEBIA *puts sugar in a cup, fills it with tea, stirs it.* NAMATA *comes back.* ZEBIA *gives her the cup and points to table. She takes it, kneels down, and places it on table. Meanwhile,* MWEBE *tries to shake the little dress clean.*

ZEBIA: It's no good trying to get it clean now. It'll have to be rewashed. (NAMATA *tiptoes to chair and takes up the clothes. As she is tiptoeing out, her father throws the soiled garment to her.*)

MWEBE (*looking at the cup and then at the tray by* ZEBIA): Good heavens, am I the only person who wants tea?

ZEBIA (*putting sugar in cups*): Namata. (NAMATA *does not answer, but appears at the door.*)

MWEBE: Why don't you answer when you are called?

ZEBIA: Bring the nuts.

MWEBE: Where are those boys? Why do they always have to be called?

ZEBIA: I don't want them to come unless their tea is ready because Tomasi might make a row.

MWEBE (*switching on the radio*): The new Saza Chief is coming to tea with the Salis on Friday.

ZEBIA: How lovely! Then the children will be able to see him. Better go and call them, Namata. They'll be thrilled! (NAMATA *goes out.*)

MWEBE: What did you say?

ZEBIA: I said the children will be able to see the new Saza Chief. They were very disappointed when I wouldn't let them go to the Installation Ceremony at the Headquarters last month; but really I didn't think it safe for them to go among such big crowds without a grown-up to look after them, since neither of us could go.

MWEBE: And now you suggest we go looking in at someone's window in order to see the Saza Chief, his guest.

ZEBIA: I didn't say anything about looking in at windows.

MWEBE: But that's what it comes to unless Sali and his wife have invited you among their important visitors.

ZEBIA: And I didn't say *we*; I was only suggesting it for the children.

MWEBE: 'Only suggesting it for the children'! And if I should say no?

A pause during which NAMATA, *who has obviously been listening at the door, opens it gently and returns into the room.*

MWEBE: I must get Sali to settle the question of that muvule-tree. I am sure that according to the old boundary it was in our plot of land. It is worth a lot of money and one must take care in claiming such things. I don't want to be accused of cheating afterwards.

ZEBIA: Namata, did you call the boys?

NAMATA: I did, Mother.

ZEBIA: Well, at least you can take your tea, since you are here.

MWEBE (*regulating the volume of the radio*): I am going to change this radio for a better one.

ZEBIA: Can we afford that now?

MWEBE: I'll see what I can get for this one first, and then find out how much a new one like the Salis's will cost.

ZEBIA: Musa has grown out of all his clothes now; and his teacher says he must have those books mentioned in the letter he brought last week.

MWEBE: And why can't Musa tell me about it himself?

ZEBIA: There is nothing I've said that you did not know already but seeing you needed to be reminded, I've reminded you.

MWEBE: Why do the children have to speak to me only through you?

ZEBIA *in silence takes up her mat and starts working.*

MWEBE: And these teachers demanding a new set of books every term: I have yet to see the good all these books have done Musa. (*Pause.*) Well, since there is no one to talk to, I suppose I'd better go. (*Goes out.*)

NAMATA: Mother, I told Tomasi and Musa about their tea, but they just don't want to come. (*Moving nearer.*) Mother, did Father say . . .

MWEBE *emerges from bedroom pushing his bicycle before him. He pushes it recklessly right across the room between* NAMATA *and the tray, and wheels it out.* ZEBIA *follows him with her eyes, and then takes up her mat and starts working at it to avoid meeting her daughter's inquiring look.* NAMATA, *seeing that her mother won't let her discover what she is thinking, picks up a spoon and stirs her tea. The laughter of children is heard again, cheerful and careless.* NAMATA *takes up her own mat and follows her mother's example.*

NAMATA: Why is Father always so brutal? Always hitting or shouting at somebody? Yesterday he came out and found Musa feeding the chickens; he pushed him against the wall, saying he was idle.

ZEBIA: He was not always like this.

NAMATA: But he has always been cruel. Musa says he's going to wait till Father is not about and then he's going to put a pin in his bicycle tyre. And Tomasi says he hates him. He says he only likes Mother.

ZEBIA (*musing*): I can remember a time when everything was different. We used to be happy. When Charles and you were little, he used to play with you. He used to sit you on the back of his neck and you would laugh as you bounced up and down. Both of you were more with him than with me. Don't you remember: I used to be quite jealous?

NAMATA: And Charles used to get between his legs and pretend to lift Daddy so that Daddy would take him up and swing him. And do you remember when we raced with him all the way from church and we won?

ZEBIA: He let you win.

NAMATA: You scolded him for behaving so childishly at church.

ZEBIA: He always brought something back for each one of us whenever he went away. He bought my blue sash after Musa was born, and tried to pop it in my mouth as I was yawning in bed. (*Pause.*)

NAMATA: But why did he change, Mother?

ZEBIA: He used to work in an office in town. But they gave his job to someone else who could speak better English, your father said.

NAMATA: What did Father do then?

ZEBIA: We couldn't go on living in the house near town after that. He had inherited this piece of land and this house from your grandfather. He came and mended it and cleaned the place up so as to make it more habitable, for there had been no one here since your grandfather's death the year before.

NAMATA: Yes, I remember Grandfather. I used to cry whenever he said I was his wife, but I liked him.

ZEBIA: You remember us selling the big house near town and moving to this one. He had to work very hard, and the harder he worked the more impatient he became.

NAMATA: But you too have changed, Mother. You didn't use to talk of work and being tired so often. You worked in the garden for only a short time each day. Now you stay digging for hours and hours. After lunch you used to sit sewing, and sometimes go visiting. Do you remember when you came back and found Charles with his head bleeding from a wound I had given him during a fight – that time we were playing with hoes? You stayed at home more then, or took us out with you. But now you come from the garden to cook and then go straight back to work afterwards, except when you aren't well like today.

ZEBIA: I suppose people do change. (*Laughter of children within.*)

NAMATA: If he comes and finds them shouting and laughing like that he's sure to hit somebody. He doesn't like anyone to be happy. He . . .

ZEBIA: Well, I don't like a lot of noise either. (NAMATA *stops and listens.*) What is it?

NAMATA (*softly*): I thought I heard a bicycle. (*Rising in a hurry.*) I'll go and warn them.

ZEBIA: Wait. Take these with you. (*They clear the tea things together and tidy the room quickly.*)

MWEBE (*within*): Take it and clean it. (NAMATA *disappears as* MWEBE *enters, vernacular newspaper in hand. Absolute hush.*) I thought the house was empty! Were you all sleeping or what? House of the dead. (ZEBIA *does not answer or look up.*) And why does that girl leave the room every time I come in? This is the third time I've noticed it. What was she or you doing that made her run away? (ZEBIA *looks up, then down again at her work.* MWEBE *sits down.*) Well, that man Sali wasn't in again.

This is the third time I've made a fruitless journey to his house.

ZEBIA: Well, Musa told me he is driving around with some . . .

MWEBE: Yes, he's touring the country with the new Saza Chief, his wife said. They're getting a car. He must be earning a lot. She was using an electric iron.

ZEBIA: They've been using electricity for nearly a year now. They say it's cheaper than paraffin in the long run.

MWEBE: Ha. They'll be saying they can't see how anyone can use paraffin. But that's no reason why I should do all this walking to and fro as if I was begging something from him. We're content with the little we possess. This affair of the land is as much his business as mine.

ZEBIA: His wife was here early this morning. She said they'd be calling on us some time; so you can talk it over when he comes.

MWEBE: Yes, I have to wait till it pleases him to talk to me. He was always below me in class, but because he could afford a secondary education and I couldn't, that puts him above me on the social scale! I won't have it. (*Pause, during which he looks at the newspaper while* ZEBIA *carries on with her mat-making.*) (*With a jerk*) Well, if lunch isn't coming, I'm going away without it.

ZEBIA: You hadn't told me you were going out before, had you? I'll go and get the food.

MWEBE: We can have our meals on time at least, even if we aren't educated, can't we? Surely you don't need to have gone to school to know that.

ZEBIA: I was only finishing off . . .

MWEBE: Take your time. I'm going. By the way, did you know Namata went to ask Sali's daughter to help her with her homework?

ZEBIA: She asked me if she could go, and I let her.

MWEBE: Why can't you use more sense?

ZEBIA: What do you mean? She couldn't do the work on her own. Mary finds it easier because her brother helps her; so why shouldn't I let her get help where she can? How was I to know it would be a cause for another quarrel?

MWEBE: Who's quarrelling now; it's you. You let other people
feel their superiority over us by allowing yourself to depend
on them. First you let her go and use their sewing machine;
so I take the trouble to borrow money in order to buy one.
Then you borrow that woman's sash; and now this.

ZEBIA: I don't see why Namata's work should suffer because
you are irritable and quarrelsome.

MWEBE: If we can't be content with what we have, we might
just as well . . .

ZEBIA (*raising her voice for the first time*): I'm fed up with your
moods. You seem to get more and more irritable every day.
If you only knew how hard it was on others. Your children are
terrified of you. You ask why the house is quiet. It is all your
doing. They can only laugh and play in your absence. I am fed
up. *Fed up.*

MWEBE: And I'm fed up with your stupidity. You're always
wearing that lean look of discontent; always in the same old
busuuti. You never give me meals on time; you care more for
the children than for me, and you are selfish and ignorant.

ZEBIA *is just about to retort when* NAMATA *appears. She quickly
pretends to be calm.*

NAMATA: The food is ready.

MWEBE: I don't know that I want any food. It's long past
lunch-time.

(*Blackout*)

SCENE TWO

An hour later.

A knock at the door. NAMATA *is on stage tuning the wireless, and
sees* SALI *and his wife at the door before they see her. Excited but
shy, she goes out.*

NORA: Hoodie! There doesn't seem to be anyone around,
though the radio is on.

SALI: They might be having a siesta; we don't want to disturb
them.

NORA *surveys the room with a superior eye, then sits down.*

MWEBE (*entering with some papers*): Oh, hello, sit down and make yourselves comfortable.

NORA: We have; at least I have, for I don't believe in all this formality. Well, Mwebe, there is John, and you should thank me for bringing him. But first I should have told you the greatest news. Our new car has arrived. It is . . . is it an Anglia or a Fiat, John? I can never remember these . . .

SALI: A DKW.

NORA: That's right. It arrived on Monday. We should have brought it over earlier to show you, but John busied himself here and there, and though I kept pestering him . . .

SALI: Mwebe, I want to settle that affair about the land with you.

NORA: That's right, and there was that too. So as soon as he came in I said to him, 'Whether you like it or not, you've got to see Mwebe. Three times he's been here wanting to see you without success. And they haven't seen the car, and I haven't seen Zebia for centuries.' (*To* MWEBE) How is Zebia? I always think she works too hard. Whenever I drop in in the morning I find her digging and I say to myself, this woman will shrink and die for lack of rest. I don't know what I'd be like if I worked as hard as she does.

SALI: My dear, we want to get down to work. I haven't much time, and you know we haven't had lunch.

ZEBIA (*coming in*): What, nearly three o'clock, and you say you haven't had lunch?

NORA: Well, you know John. If I let him escape once I'd got him, it would take another month to get him to come. No lunch, I said to him, till we have fulfilled our duty to our neighbours. 'Self last' is a golden rule.

ZEBIA: Well, you must be starving. I'll go and get you something to eat. It won't take long. (*Makes to go out.*)

SALI: Don't trouble, Zebia. We are not going to stay long and lunch is waiting at home.

NORA: Mwebe, don't you think Zebia looks very skinny. I was telling your husband, my dear, that what you need is rest. You work too much.

F

MWEBE: We definitely can't work here. Let's go somewhere else.

NORA: That's right, let's go out and see the car.

SALI: Right, go on. You lead the way, Nora.

NORA *goes to* ZEBIA *and whispers, taking her by the hand. They go out.*

MWEBE: Good, now to business. The Muluka Chief was asking me if the muvule-tree was mine. I couldn't give him an answer, because I wasn't sure.

SALI: Well, what do you think?

MWEBE: I know my father always said it was his. There's quite a lot of money involved, so I don't want to be accused of dishonesty afterwards.

SALI: No one is accusing you of dishonesty. I've got it all arranged. What the Muluka Chief needs is my word that I have no claim on the tree. If both of us sign this paper, all will be well. (*Gives* MWEBE *a paper.* MWEBE *reads it, signs it, and hands it back in silence.* SALI *goes over it thoughtfully.*)

NORA (*off-stage*): John! You didn't lock the car. You're so forgetful.

SALI: I didn't think it was necessary to lock it.

NORA: You should always lock it. Didn't you hear the man say that if you didn't develop the habit, you might find yourself in trouble one day.

SALI (*throwing her the key*): Well, there, go and lock it.

NORA: Anyway, we ought to be going.

SALI: Yes, if you'll let us finish this business. (NORA *disappears.*) That woman is the plague of my life. She wants this, that and the other thing: she must always have her own way. She forced me to send the children to boarding school, saying they couldn't go to day school like everyone else's. It's getting too expensive for me. For two years she's been pestering me to get a car, until I got so fed up that I had to borrow money to buy one, and then she wouldn't let me buy a second-hand one. I don't think I can afford to run a car, let alone pay a debt on top of that. Don't be surprised if I end up in prison.

MWEBE: Well, why didn't you explain to her all about your money problems, and how much the car would cost?

SALI: It's not easy to explain; you know what I mean. When they see you going to work every morning, they think you must be rolling in money.

MWEBE: Do you mean to say she doesn't actually know how much you earn?

SALI: What do you mean, man? Do you think a sensible fellow like me could tell his wife, of all women, about his salary and all that?

MWEBE: Well, how else is she to know whether you can afford a car or not?

NORA (*within*): John, do hurry up. I'm starving, and you told Zebia not to give us food, saying we wouldn't be long.

SALI: I suppose all women are like that. (*Goes out, followed by* MWEBE.)

Children laugh offstage.

MWEBE (*comes in and throws himself on a chair, shaking his head*): Lord, what a woman! I wouldn't keep a wife like that for all the fine cars and houses in the world.

NAMATA (*runs in still laughing*): Mother, mother, come and see . . . *She realizes that her mother is not in the room. She and her father look at each other. She seems to be looking for the best way to leave the room.*

MWEBE: Do you want Mother to come? What is it you want her to see?

NAMATA (*doubtfully*): Musa's car . . . with some people in it.

MWEBE: Ask Musa to bring it and show me.

NAMATA: But he has drawn it on the ground outside. (*Pause.*)

MWEBE: May I come and see it?

NAMATA: Yes.

Goes out followed by her father. Curtain as they go out.

Tunde Aiyegbusi

LADIPO'S LAST STAND

A play in one act

CHARACTERS

MR LANRE LADIPO
MRS LADIPO
TUNDE – *their son*
LAIDE – *their daughter*
MR COKER – *a Councillor*

Scene: MR LADIPO'*s sitting-room. On the wall hangs a portrait of
an old man. When the curtain opens,* MR LADIPO *is revealed stirring
his cup of cocoa.* MRS LADIPO *is sitting on a low chair to her
husband's right, near the door, darning a dress.*

MR LADIPO (*studying his wrist-watch*): I wonder what's happened.

MRS LADIPO: Happened?

MR LADIPO: Yes. Tunde isn't back yet. In fact he's almost an
hour overdue. The interview was supposed to take place at
nine this morning. And he promised to be back for cocoa.

MRS LADIPO: Yes, he did. Oh well, maybe the interview
dragged on longer than usual. You know our people. You
know what they're like when it comes to a thing like that.

MR LADIPO: Do they need a whole day to interview a person?
What efficiency! Look, the Kano train arrived an hour ago and
yet no sign of him.

A VOICE: Father! Here's a letter, here's a letter for you.

The voice is LAIDE'*s,* MR LADIPO'*s daughter, a girl of eighteen. She gives a letter to* MR LADIPO.

MR LADIPO: Laide, did your brother tell you that he wouldn't be back today?

LAIDE: No, Father. He promised to be back for cocoa. I'm surprised he didn't come by the last train.

MR LADIPO (*who has ripped the envelope open*): Hm . . . Hm . . . What . . . What . . .? I can't make head or tail of these scratches. One would have thought they kept spiders as clerks to write their letters. Laide, read me what the idiots have to say. (*Takes the cup of cocoa and sips.*)

LAIDE (*reading aloud*): 'Town Planning Division . . .'

MR LADIPO: I know where it comes from. Just read me what the morons have to say.

LAIDE: 'Sir,

With reference to your letter of the 5th instant, I am directed to inform you that your objections to development plan C/B/15 have been duly considered by the Town Planning Division. They note that your house is scheduled for demolition and regret that this may cause some inconvenience to you and your family. However, adequate compensation has been offered, and so I am accordingly directed to inform you that the Council's decision must be implemented and that you are required to vacate the said premises by the 16th of May.

Yours faithfully . . .

Meanwhile MRS LADIPO *has gradually stopped her work and, at the last bit of information, her hands drop to her lap.*

MR LADIPO (*sarcastically*): Listen to the voice of our local gods! 'Council's decision must be implemented.' What on earth do they take me for? This is really a big joke. I tell you they're fooling no one but themselves. No. I've suffered enough for the 'common good'. It's scarcely a year now since they took away my land to build the Youth Camp. Of course, I had to give in then. There was no choice. And now it's my house and, as always, for the 'common good'. Must I be the only sufferer? Can't someone else make a little sacrifice for once; for me? This time they've staked on the wrong horse. No-one; no

Council, not even the 'common good' is going to deprive me of my home. I'll see to that.

MRS LADIPO: I don't understand. Are the Authorities talking again about the demolition?

MR LADIPO: Yes . . . and they've given us a time-limit too! We've got a month to look for alternative accommodation. What a way to put it.

LAIDE (*horrified*): A month? Where on earth can one get a house at such short notice in this crazy town? They're out of their minds. Surely, they don't expect us to live in the slums, and where else is there?

MR LADIPO: Don't they? They don't care tuppence if we all have to sleep in the gutter.

MRS LADIPO: But this is the most callous thing to talk of doing.

MR LADIPO: But they'll do it all the same. They commit the very worst crimes and they claim they are doing everything for 'the common good'. Take my farm for example. It was just the same. Didn't these same men grab that fertile piece of land and convert it into a resort of idleness for the sons and daughters of nobodies? Did they spare a thought for me or my family? Not on their lives. For them it's do unto others what you'd hate them to do unto you.

MRS LADIPO: But have we no friends? What about Councillor Coker? Surely we can rely on him. *He* won't allow this to happen to us.

MR LADIPO (*contemptuously*): Coker! Heh, how can you think so highly of such men? Coker is a thoroughly rotten egg. They're all alike. They all croak alike, just like frogs before a storm. Your Councillor Coker knows far too well which side his bread is buttered to do anything for us.

MRS LADIPO: That can't possibly be true, Lanre. I think you're being very unfair to him.

MR LADIPO: You don't believe me, do you? You wait and see.

MRS LADIPO: Have you consulted the D.O.? He's a nice fellow and very understanding. At least that's everybody's opinion of him.

MR LADIPO: I suppose he's understanding when he chooses to

be. But apparently this is one instance where he prefers to be impervious to reason. He's no better than all the rest of them – in spite of what everybody says.

LAIDE: But, Father, there are three boys on his scholarships at Training College, and . . .

MR LADIPO (*interrupting*): Does that make him a reasonable man? It only shows he can afford it. After all, it's *our* money. (*To* MRS LADIPO.) Anyway, I have been to him. I put our case to him several times and he's no use. The last time I was with him, he kept on preaching to me of the good in having a well-planned city with drainage and all that – as though I were an idiot. Your D.O. is merely a useful tool in the hands of your Councillors – a 'Yes' man.

MRS LADIPO: What about making a fresh approach to him? Surely we can get him to see our point of view. I'll go along with you.

MR LADIPO: No. A hundred times, no! I know my rights and I'm not going to beg for them.

MRS LADIPO: Let *me* go then. We women have a way of getting what we want, you know. It's a feminine secret. Do let me go. I know I could do something.

MR LADIPO: You're not to go a step outside that door. If you do, you'll never come into this room again.

MRS LADIPO (*heaving a sigh*): Well, if the Council is bent on having its own way, if the D.O. chooses to back them, and if you won't let me try to help, I don't see what else we can do.

MR LADIPO: You too?

MRS LADIPO: What about me?

MR LADIPO: You want me to allow those dogs to destroy every-thing we have. You want me to be the spineless offspring of a noble name? You want . . .

LAIDE: Father!

MRS LADIPO: Don't get so worked up, dear. I don't want you to be any other thing than my good husband and the loving father that you are.

MR LADIPO: How can I be sure of that? You don't sound as though you believed it. Do you realize what it will mean

if we give in? I don't suppose you've thought about it for a
moment.

MRS LADIPO: Dear, you must understand me. I think the mark
of honour is in knowing when you're beaten. As things stand,
this surely isn't a fight we can win. And I shudder to imagine
you setting yourself up against the Authorities.

MR LADIPO (*indignantly*): The Authorities my foot! If Authority
only speaks the language of force, what hinders me from speaking the same tongue?

LAIDE: Father, I think Mama is right.

MR LADIPO: Think what you like, child. But why should the
Council deprive me of my rights? They have no authority to
turn me out. They can only do it by force.

LAIDE: Ye-e-s, but it's not only the Authorities we're up against.
Think of the people too. Everyone would say it's you who
opposes everything progressive the Council plans for the
Community. All the good you've done would be forgotten.
And when the Council ultimately wins, there'll be no sym-
pathy left for you . . . anywhere. Have you thought of that,
Father?

MR LADIPO: No, no, child. You talk of the people. Am I an
animal? Am I not one of the people? I see you don't understand. Listen, Laide. This is a fight we must win or worse
things will follow. Do you think I voted for these men to have
myself stripped of everything I cherish? They're doing these
things to me because they think I'm powerless . . . Yes, they
think I'm powerless. But they'd better not be so sure.

LAIDE: Don't get so worked up, Father. Perhaps the Council
may still alter its mind about the order.

MRS LADIPO: Besides, Tunde will surely fight them for you.
They'll know then what it is to have an educated man for a son.
Where old age fails, youth may well succeed, you know.

A brief silence. A knock is heard. LAIDE *stands to clear the stools.
She quickly packs up the kettle and the cups but on second thoughts
replaces them and makes for the door. A second knock harder than
the first.*

MRS LADIPO: Come right in, please!

A middle-aged man in a black suit and an old tie done up in a bundle of a knot enters. He removes his hat as he bows to MRS LADIPO. *He is* MR COKER – *a Town Councillor.*

MR COKER: Good evening, Madam.

MRS LADIPO: Good evening, Mr Coker. How's everybody at home? What a long time since we've seen you. Anybody would think we had offended you. We haven't, have we?

MR COKER: Oh no, not at all. It's all this Council business. You see, we have so many eggs on our plate just now – I mean in the committees. There's just too much to be done. Would you believe it; sometimes we sit as late as twelve midnight? I have kept away today because my health simply wouldn't stand it.

MRS LADIPO: Twelve midnight? Whatever are you discussing till that hour? I'm happy I succeeded in persuading Lanre not to contest the elections. I can't afford to be without my man for so long. Tell me, how does Bimpe bear it all? Poor woman! Anyway, Mr Coker, I'm very happy to see that at last we have really dedicated men at the helm, who are prepared to devote their lives to the work.

MR LADIPO (*who does not share his wife's enthusiasm*): Do you think so? *I* can't say as much for our dedicated overlords.

MR COKER: Of course, that's the unhappy lot of public figures. It's humanly impossible to please everybody.

MR LADIPO: That's no defence, Mr Coker.

MRS LADIPO (*eager to prevent any unpleasantness*): Oh, Mister Coker, please make yourself comfortable (*pointing to an empty chair*). Now tell me about the children. How's our Remi? I'm told she's very much like her mother. Bimpe loathes calling on neighbours, you know, and we hardly ever see her. (*The Councillor smiles uncertainly.*) Laide, make some cocoa for the Councillor.

Exit LAIDE. MR LADIPO *slowly walks up to the table, picks up the letter and hands it to* MR COKER.

MR LADIPO: Read that, and tell me what you think of it.

MR COKER *is surprised by the cold hostility in his host's voice, stares uncomprehendingly at him for a while and then proceeds to read the letter. He nods pointlessly as he reads every sentence. He folds the*

G

*letter and puts it in his pocket. He realizes his mistake; quickly
retrieves the paper and holds it undecidedly between his fingers, eyes
fixed on the ceiling.*

MR LADIPO: Well?

MR COKER: When, if I may ask, did you get this?

MR LADIPO: What has that got to do with what's in it, Mr
Coker?

MR COKER: This is all most unfortunate. I'm terribly sorry
about the whole unpleasant business.

MR LADIPO: Sorry? (*Laughs derisively.*) Are you really sorry?
Are you denying responsibility for what you've done, Mr
Coker? Am I to understand that there isn't any justification
whatsoever for this iniquitous attempt to pull down my
house? Are you insinuating that the Council has nothing to do
with it? Are you . . .

MRS LADIPO (*checking her husband*): Lanre! (*She sees* LAIDE
coming through the door.) Laide, put it here for Mister Coker.
LAIDE *places the cup and kettle on the stool in front of* MR COKER;
exchanges glances with her mother and goes out.

MR COKER (*pouring out the cocoa*): Mr Ladipo, I want you to
realize that this . . . very unfortunate business hits me as hard
as it hits you. Do you think I am so bad as to dine and wine
with you and yet support any move calculated to harm you.
God forbid! (*He sips some cocoa; finds it too hot and hastily puts the
cup back onto the saucer.*) You see, the first time this matter came
up for discussion, you can't imagine now furious I was. I was
on my feet for more than a solid hour speaking against it . . .

MRS LADIPO: There you are, Lanre, what did I say? I told you
Mr Coker would be the last person to favour such a move.

MR COKER: . . . and I carried the whole Council with me that
day. But at the second meeting, it was different. The D.O.
spoke at length of epidemics, sanitation and the elegance of a
well-planned city. The result was that at the end of his speech
I was the lone opposer of the motion.

MR LADIPO: And so . . . you've joined the chorus too.

MR COKER: You have to understand my plight. Put yourself in
my position. What would you have done?

MR LADIPO: You really want to know? Then listen carefully I would have walked out on them there and then and damn the consequences. Yes; that's what I'd have done. But you? No! I can understand your plight as you call it. You wouldn't have had the guts to do that. You don't care what happens to other people as long as your pockets are full. And if you stood up against them, it might affect business. Am I very wrong, Mister Councillor?

MR COKER: I'm not in the least prepared for this sort of — Mr Ladipo, you're behaving very oddly tonight. (*To* MRS LADIPO): Thanks. It was such a nice cup of cocoa. I think I should be going. It's getting late and I still have to pay some calls.

MR LADIPO (*as* MR COKER *makes for the door*): So you're exactly like all the rest of them. I see, Mr Coker! (*The Councillor turns to face* MR LADIPO.) You think you can lick me with your dishonest manœuvres. But this won't be by any means as easy as the last time. I'm going to put up a fight: the greatest fight of my life. Have you ever watched a cornered snake fight for it's life? You're going to see something really tough. Even if I fall in the thick of this, there's Tunde to carry on the struggle.

A young man enters. He is neatly dressed in a European suit; he has a Lenin-style beard which gives him an air of responsibility in spite of his youthful features.

MRS LADIPO (*embracing the new-comer*): Welcome, Tunde. We've all been expecting you. Your father was rather worried about you. Did you come by the Kano train?

TUNDE: I missed that. The interview was over in the morning, but the Recruitment Officer wanted me to wait for the result. By the time all the formalities were over, I knew I couldn't possibly be at the station in time to catch the Kano train.

MRS LADIPO: How did you travel, then? Did you come down by lorry? Tunde, but I warned you . . .

TUNDE: Oh, no. I didn't travel by lorry. I took the Offa train. I was terribly lucky to get to the station in time for it. Where's Laide?

MRS LADIPO: She's in the kitchen. I must go and help her with the food. Excuse me, Mr Coker.

Exit MRS LADIPO. *Tunde moves to a chair; turns, and discovers the Councillor.*

TUNDE: Good evening, Mr Coker!

MR COKER: 'Devening Tunde. Nice to see you again.

TUNDE: Don't let me interrupt you. Do sit down.

MR COKER: No, really, I should be going. As a matter of fact, I was about to leave when you came in.

TUNDE: You don't mean to say you're going away – when I've just come. You can't do that. Do sit down (*pushes the chair nearest* MR COKER *to him*).

MR LADIPO: Well? How did the interview go?

TUNDE: Successful. Completely successful. I'm starting work on Monday. So I'm paying a month's salary to the Railways in lieu of notice.

MR COKER: Congratulations! It joys my heart to hear of your success.

MR LADIPO: I've never doubted your success, son. My only fear was of the men that governed our destiny. I'm now convinced that the rulers over there are not like the vampires we have here. (*Pause.*) Where will you be stationed? I very much hope you aren't going to be miles away from civilization.

TUNDE: No, Father. I'm remaining here. I'm going to be works' engineer for our local Council. I shall be in charge of Town Planning. My first assignment is the implementation of the new scheme for the town. You can imagine how thrilled I am that I'm going to have a hand in creating a new look for our area. It's long overdue.

MR COKER (*wildly excited*): Congratulations! So you're to take Mr Tate's place. Wonderful! Terrific! Simply marvellous! So at last our son is to be the works' engineer! That's what we've wished for all these years.

MR LADIPO (*dazed, slowly rising from his seat*): Surely I didn't hear you. Did you say you were going to be in charge of the ... Town Planning Scheme?

TUNDE: Of course, Dad. And this is only the beginning.

There'll be many more. We'll make this old place so fine she won't know herself. Already I've an idea . . .

MR LADIPO: Stop! Shut up! Do you know what you're saying?

TUNDE: Why? What do you mean?

MR LADIPO: I said 'Stop'!

TUNDE: I don't understand.

MR LADIPO: You don't understand. No – that's your only excuse. Have you thought for one moment what evil you're getting yourself involved in?

TUNDE: Evil? What do you mean, Dad? This is something good and useful. Haven't you always said you wanted me to be useful to our people?

MR LADIPO: Yes, of course, I want you to be useful. But I didn't work myself to the bone to educate you in order that you could destroy the happiness of your own people. Can't you find another job?

TUNDE: What's wrong with this?

MR LADIPO: Nothing. (*Thundering*) But I don't like it. And I don't want you to have anything to do with it. You understand me?

TUNDE: But, Father, this is an opportunity that must not be allowed to slip through our fingers.

MR LAPIDO: Opportunity my foot! Do you realize what you're letting yourself in for? You're being entrusted with the task of destroying your own home. Read that – (*he hands the letter and waits with barely concealed impatience while* TUNDE *reads it*).

TUNDE: But, Father, the government is offering good compensation. With that we can buy a new piece of land and build another house – the most modern type. This old shell wouldn't have lasted much longer, anyway.

MR COKER: And that's not to mention the public appreciation of your sacrifice.

MR LADIPO: I care neither for your compensation nor what your foolish public thinks of me. Tunde, listen to me. For your own sake, you should wash your hands of this crazy job.

TUNDE: You haven't made clear why I should, Father.

MR LADIPO: Do you remember that my land was taken by this

same Council and given to the children of pot-bellied non-entities?

MR COKER: No, no. I really must interrupt. The last statement was grossly inaccurate. It's not only the children of pot-bellied nonentities that use the camp. My children go there and many eminent citizens' . . .

MR LADIPO (*ignoring the Councillor*): And now these men are forcing me to quit my house. You don't need a god to tell you that this is a conspiracy. They're out to hunt me down. But, conspiracy or not, never mind, we're strong enough for them.

TUNDE: Father, no one is hunting anyone down. It just happens that our own house is the one involved this time. It could have been anybody's. Nobody is being persecuted. It's purely accidental that this happens to be *our* house.

MR LADIPO: 'Purely accidental'! I see there's little to choose between you with your education and these ignorant Councillors. As far as they're concerned, nothing ever happens for a good reason. It's always purely accidental. Tunde, I'm ashamed of you.

TUNDE: Father, I wasn't expecting objections like this. You've taken me completely by surprise. I don't understand. To listen to what you're saying now, no one would imagine that you were one of those who accused the Council of ignoring this area. Over and over again you have demanded that they do something for us. And now that your sustained complaints are yielding fruit, you're blocking the way. I just don't understand it.

MR LADIPO: I ought to have guessed this is what would happen. You're with them, aren't you? You want the graves of your ancestors violated and their peace disturbed. Do you think they will thank you for the roar of motor cars and fumes of petrol choking them for twenty-four hours in the day? Is that the sort of rest you pray for? Is this the return you expect from your issue? Think of what you're doing. Think . . . think . . . think before it's too late.

TUNDE: What's all this? Oh, Father, don't you see these are just excuses. I'm doing nothing I'll be ashamed of. In fact, we may very well have cause to be proud of our part in this. It's a chance of a lifetime. Father, just imagine the new street, broad, clean, tarmac'd and brilliantly lit! Think of what this could have meant years ago. I'm inclined to believe our ancestors will prefer cleanliness and gaiety to filth and dung.

MR COKER: And if I may say so, this road will be a fitting memorial to the Ladipo family. A good name is better ... ..

MR LADIPO: Spare us your shallow philosophy, Mr Councillor.

TUNDE: Father, what do you expect me to do? I thought about this job very carefully. I weighed the merits before I accepted it.

MR LADIPO: If you have an ounce of honour left, you will have nothing to do with this – this obnoxious project. Let someone else undertake it. Then it will be easier for us to fight the common enemy . . . together.

TUNDE: But, Father, you can't mean it. You can't possibly want that. This is a chance we mustn't miss.

MR LADIPO: Get out of here! (*Advancing towards* TUNDE *and* MR COKER) Both of you! (*Enter* MRS LADIPO *and* LAIDE *carrying a tray of food.*) Go and join forces. I'll beat you yet, yes, the whole pack of you.

MRS LADIPO: What's all this about?

MR LADIPO: It's about your son.

MRS LADIPO: Tunde? Whatever can be the matter?

MR LADIPO: It's simply that he thinks he knows what's good for everyone. Even for his own father. He's with the Council. He's my enemy.

MRS LADIPO: With the Council! That's impossible.

MR COKER: In point of fact, Tunde didn't quite mean it like that.

MRS LADIPO: Tunde, come here a minute. Laide, we aren't ready for the food yet. Take it back. (*Exit* LAIDE.) Now, Tunde, you know it's very bad for your father to get so excited. Humour him a little.

TUNDE: But, Mother, he's making things so difficult for me. He simply won't listen to a word I say.

MRS LADIPO: Of course he won't listen if you aren't tactful. Oh

dear, you two are far too like each other. Now talk to him
quietly. Let him see your reasons and if he still wants you to
fight them, you will help him, son, won't you?

TUNDE: I don't think I can promise that, Mother; but I'll try to
persuade him.

He goes to MR LADIPO *who, all this time, has been looking at the
picture on the wall; while* MR COKER *sits uneasily watching one
after the other.*

TUNDE: Father . . . Father, please listen to me. For your own
sake, for my sake, for the sake of progress, let's . . .

MR LADIPO (*sarcastically*): Let's do what, my dear son?

TUNDE: I mean, let's give the Council a free hand in this
business.

MR LADIPO: Thank you. That may be what you think, Mr
Know-all. But not me. No. Not for any reasonable man either.
I expected such soft talk from a woman. Not from a man. I
pity the woman that marries the likes of you. You! You who
can't stand up for yourself, so how can you . . .

MRS LADIPO: Lanre! Don't say such things. It's bad.

MR LADIPO: Bad, eh? But it isn't bad for a son to take his father,
his own father, for a fool? It isn't bad when a son neglects the
rightful duties of a son? Tell me, what's good about that?

MRS LADIPO: Lanre, this isn't the way to behave to your own
son. Tunde isn't very old yet. He's really only a small boy.
He needs more time to realize all you're saying. Please, please
give him time.

MR COKER: And there's no doubt, Mr Ladipo, that there's an
element of error in your judgment of the present situation.
The power in this present case rests with the Council and the
Council alone. Your son is only the Council's employee. Mr
Ladipo, if I may say so, you are channelling your fighting
energy in the wrong direction. Even if Tunde gives up the
job, it won't stop the house being demolished.

MR LADIPO: When I want your advice I'll ask for it, Mr
Councillor. (*To* MRS LADIPO) You call this a small boy?
You're cursing him. People younger than him have fathered
children. If he's small now, he'll never grow up. Never. Never.

At his age, I knew what was right. I knew it and stood by it. I see now why my father didn't want me to have the white-man's education. (*Pointing at* TUNDE) This is the result. The old man knew what he was talking about. I've been nothing but a fool.

TUNDE: Father, please listen to me. Let's give the Council a chance. Our elders used to say that a solitary tree stands in danger in even the weakest storm. Father, don't make yourself that solitary tree. After all, there's the compensation and . . .

MR LADIPO: Who told you that rubbish? Which stupid elders believe in that sort of nonsense. No elder that is a man gives his ears to such cowards' philosophy. Isn't the iroko, the king of trees, a lone stander? C'mon, think of a better lie to cover your shame. (*He goes to the portrait and contemplates.*) This behaviour of yours will make the old man turn in his grave. (*Casting an accusing glance at his wife*) O that a lion should beget a sheep. This is a shame, the greatest shame!

TUNDE: This isn't a question of shame. It's a clear case of realizing what's possible, what's proper.

MR LADIPO: And you do? You weakling! I'm happy you've shown yourself in your true colours early enough, before I ever thought I could lean on you. Why did God punish me with a disgrace like you?

MR COKER: Mr Ladipo, I must confess that I'm totally non-plussed by this uncompromising attitude of yours. You ought to realize that it's an uphill task pitching yourself against constituted authority, having all the support and confidence of the whole populace behind it.

MR LADIPO: So you think your power entitles you to run me down like an earthworm. I'll show you how wrong you are. For this once, you're all going to realize to your shame that there's at least one real man left.

TUNDE: Father, I fear for you. This isn't the right stand to take. Remember that the Council can proceed with the plan without your consent.

MR LADIPO: Good. Let them dare. And let me tell you that I

need no advice from you or anyone else. I took decisions
before you were born.

MR COKER: Obviously; but times have changed Mr Ladipo.

MRS LADIPO: Lanre, what's come over you? Talking like that to
your own son. Whoever heard of such behaviour?

MR LADIPO: This my son? No. A coward never will be my son.
No true Ladipo is a coward. This is the Council's son. Get
out. Get out of here, you contemptible, spineless, shameless . . .

MRS LADIPO: Lanre!

TUNDE *measures his father with a contemptuous look and makes for
his bag. At the door, he turns to have a last look at him.*

TUNDE: You can't say I didn't warn you. (*Exit.*)

MRS LADIPO (*shouting after* TUNDE): Tunde, Tunde . . . don't
go away. Come back here. (*Turns to her husband with a dejected
look*) Oh dear!

MR COKER: Mr Ladipo, I'm cocksure you'll come round, at last,
to appreciate our point. It's simply inevitable. (*Moving away.*)
However, if I can still be of help in any way whatsoever, I'm
always at your service.

MR LADIPO (*collapsing in his chair*): You aren't going to have
that joy; take that from me. (*Exit* MR COKER.)

MRS LADIPO: Lanre, I can't understand this. It's beyond me.
Oh, how I wish I knew what to do. But I just can't understand
it at all. (*Pause.*) Tell me, what will you do now?

MR LADIPO (*holding on to his wife's hand*): Prepare for their
coming.

CURTAIN

Peter Nazareth

BRAVE NEW COSMOS

CHARACTERS

KAGGWA – *an undergraduate*
KARANJA – *an undergraduate – later a graduate*
KIWANUKA – *a teacher*
CHORUS – *the audience*

SCENE ONE

An undergraduate's room, very neat yet bare. It contains only necessary items of furniture. A bed is on the right. To the left of the bed is a writing-table and a chair. Next to the writing-table is a cupboard. On some of the shelves of this cupboard are many books. KAGGWA *is sitting at the table, writing. He is dressed neatly; he is wearing a white shirt, grey trousers and a tie. A knock is heard. No answer. Another knock is heard, louder. Again no answer. A knock so loud that the walls threaten to collapse. Still no answer.* KARANJA *walks in fuming. He is dressed just like* KAGGWA. *He takes a few determined steps and stops a few yards from* KAGGWA.

KARANJA: Didn't you hear me knocking?

KAGGWA (*without looking up*): Shh. Please do not make a noise. I am writing an essay for Mr Brown.

KARANJA: Now see here, Kaggwa, I've waited long enough . . .

KAGGWA (*looking up*): A great critic said, 'All the things that, to the human spirit, are most profoundly significant, can only be experienced, not expressed. The rest is always and everywhere silence.' So please – keep – quiet.

KARANJA (*grabbing* KAGGWA *by the scruff of his neck and pulling him to his feet. Shouts*): I've waited long enough for you to repay the money you've borrowed from me. You've borrowed ten shillings so far! Now, are you going to return my money, or do I have to break your miserable neck?

KAGGWA (*struggling free. Fingering his neck gingerly, then smoothing his tie*): Shakespeare says:

'Neither a borrower, nor a lender be;
    For loan oft loses both itself and friend.'

When I asked you for money, you should have refused.

KARANJA (*turning away, clenching his fists and gritting his teeth*): Oh!

KAGGWA: Look here, Karanja, I know I've borrowed some money from you, but can't you have any patience? I'll repay you even if it takes me a lifetime to do so.

KARANJA: What – a lifetime? (*He takes a threatening step towards* KAGGWA, *who jumps back.*) But I need the money desperately: I need it now! I have to clear my bill at the bar or I'll get into serious trouble!

KAGGWA: That's your business, not mine. When you lent me the money I didn't tell you when I would repay it. (*Pointing to the door.*) 'Out, damned spot, out I say!' Or else keep quiet, because I want to finish this essay. (*Sits down.*)

KARANJA (*turning away helplessly*): Keep quiet, he says! He borrows cash from me – why? So that he can impress his girl. So that he can take her to the pictures and to dances: so that he can buy her little gifts. He comes up to me and pleads with me: 'Karanja, you're my best friend. You simply must help me!' So what can I do? (*Turning abruptly and walking towards* KAGGWA *with hands outstretched*) But I'll get my money back from you if I have to skin you alive. I'll break every bone in your miserable body. (*His hands are closing round* KAGGWA's *neck when* KAGGWA *suddenly becomes aware of this new threat. He jumps up in alarm and backs away from* KARANJA, *who follows him with hands outstretched.*)

KAGGWA: Now, my good sir, you really mustn't . . .

KARANJA (*more frustrated than angry*): I'll suck your blood. I'll use your skin to make drums, as our ancestors did.

KAGGWA (*backing away*): 'Are you fantastical?'

KARANJA's hands close on KAGGWA's throat. KAGGWA wrenches himself free and runs out shouting, 'Help – there's a maniac in my room'.

KARANJA (*shouting after KAGGWA hopelessly*): But I need the money desperately! Oh, what's the use. He comes to me and says, 'Karanja, brother, I would like to treat you to a drink in the canteen'. We have a long friendly talk over a few bottles of beer, a talk punctuated by, 'You're my best friend, Karanja.' Then he asks for a loan. (*Sits on a chair hopelessly.*) When I want the money back, he says (*springing up*) 'Tomorrow and to-morrow and . . .' All he can do is spout quotations. Oh, how I hate these arts students! No, I'm *not* your best friend, Kaggwa! I'll get my money back from you somehow. (*Begins searching the shelves of the cupboard, upsetting all the books. Then pulls out KAGGWA's suitcase from under the bed and searches through it, flinging the clothes on to the bed. A knock is heard.*)

KARANJA (*unthinkingly*): Come in.

KIWANUKA walks in. He is wearing brown trousers, a coloured shirt, and a sweater.

KIWANUKA: Er – good evening.

(*KARANJA jumps up, hearing this unfamiliar voice. He turns round, suddenly embarrassed.*

KIWANUKA: I was told that this is where Mr Kaggwa stays.

KARANJA: That's right. Mr Kaggwa does stay here.

KIWANUKA: Oh, do you share this room?

KARANJA: Not exactly . . . I – er, that is – er, Mr Kaggwa . . . He just went out to buy a packet of cigarettes. I'll call him for you. You sit here. (*He gives him the chair, practically forcing him on to it. Then KARANJA rushes out; and rushes back to push the clothes into the suitcase. He rushes out again; but stops in the doorway.*) I'll be back in a minute, Mr – er —

He leaves just before KIWANUKA answers.

KIWANUKA (*bewildered*): Kiwanuka, an old friend of Mr

Kaggwa's. This is very strange. Is this really how the intelli-
gentsia behave? (*Shakes his head.*) Maybe I am out of touch
with the present. (*Gets up to look at the books.*) Hmm – *Hamlet,
Macbeth, The Tempest, Poems of Wordsworth* . . . a very good
collection of books.

KARANJA *and* KAGGWA *walk in.*

KAGGWA: Er –

KIWANUKA *turns round.*

KIWANUKA: Why, Kaggwa!

KAGGWA: Who are you?

KIWANUKA: Why, Kiwanuka, your old classmate. Remember,
we were in the same class in 1957.

KAGGWA (*hesitantly*): Sit down, sit down. (*To* KARANJA)
Please sit down, Mr Karanja. (KAGGWA *sits on the bed,*
KARANJA *the table.*)

KIWANUKA: Well, Kaggwa, how are you these days? I haven't
seen you since we finished school. (*Sadly.*) Of course, I didn't
do so well in my exam as to be able to come to this wonderful
place. You did very well. (*Laughs.*) You always were the
studious one in our class. You thought games and out-of-
school activities were a waste of time. You wanted to play an
important part in life. You said, 'I want to become a graduate –
and then the world will be at my feet!' You were right, of
course. Here you are in the University of East Africa – everybody's dream.

KAGGWA: Yes, I told you that I was right, but you never
believed me! You didn't think that studying was the important
thing if one wanted to get on in life.

KIWANUKA: What are you reading in this University?

KAGGWA: I am *studying* for an arts degree. I can never understand why the lecturers here prefer the word 'reading' to the
word 'studying'. One not only reads in a university – one
studies. The average man who isn't clever enough to gain
admission into a university 'reads': he reads ordinary novels,
newspapers, and all kinds of cheap literature. (*Points proudly to
his books.*) I *study* – these plays and poems.

KIWANUKA: I like Shakespeare very much, too. I like *Hamlet*

very much because it is very true to life. Oh, I recently read a
very interesting article on Shakespeare in the *Time Magazine*.

KAGGWA: *Time Magazine? Time Magazine?* That trash! How
could any news magazine write a good article on Shakespeare?
No. I read and study the great books of criticism like Bradley's.
Not only that (*pulling out a little red notebook*), I note down
important quotations from the great critics. For instance
(*thumbing through his book*), did you know that Bradley said,
(*reading*) 'I have dwelt thus at length on Hamlet's melancholy
because, from the psychological point of view, it is the centre
of the tragedy, and to omit it from consideration or to underrate
its intensity is to make Shakespeare's story unintelligible'?

KARANJA *yawns out loudly.*

KARANJA (*apologetically*): Pardon me.

KIWANUKA (*turning round*): You haven't introduced me to your
friend.

KAGGWA: Kiwanuka, this is Karanja. Karanja, this is Kiwanuka.
(*They shake hands.*) Karanja is a very good friend of mine. We
are such good friends that we often lend each other money and
never bother about asking for it back. For instance, Karanja
now owes me ten shillings but I don't ask him to repay it.

KARANJA (*jumping up*): Wha—?

KAGGWA: No, no, don't bother to express your gratitude.
'To be honest, as this world goes, is to be one man picked out
of ten thousand!'

KARANJA: I appeal to you, Mr Kiwanuka. Kaggwa is the one
who always borrows money from *me*. At the moment, *he* owes
me ten shillings. I need this money desperately but he won't
pay it back!

KAGGWA: But I can't . . .

KIWANUKA (*taking out his wallet and drawing out a ten-shilling note*):
I'll give you the money. (*To* KAGGWA) That's just for old
time's sake. When you graduate and when you're a big man,
maybe you can pay it back.

KARANJA *kisses the money and is rushing out wild with joy when
he suddenly remembers himself and comes back to his old position.*

KARANJA: Thank you, Kiwanuka.

KAGGWA: Er, thank you. (*Quotes*):
'Oft expectation fails, and most oft there
Where most it promises.'

KIWANUKA (*to* KAGGWA): And what are you reading here, Mr
Karanja?

KARANJA: Well, I am *studying* science. I don't believe in wasting
my time like my friend here – reading (*contemptuously*) Shakespeare, Wordsworth, Aristotle – phooey! What does it matter
if Shakespeare said stupid things like, 'To be or not to be'? Let
Shakespeare say what he wants to say, but I'm not going to
study that rubbish.

KIWANUKA: Well, science is very useful, no doubt, but
surely . . .

KARANJA: 'Let Nature teach you!' Ugh! Wordsworth! How has
this world progressed? By means of what Shakespeare said?
There weren't any motor cars in his day, no record-players, no
radios. He had no cinemas; I go to see at least three pictures a
week. How has the world progressed? By science – science is
the all-powerful god! Why should I read Shakespeare when he
didn't even know that H_2SO_4 plus Z_n equals Z_nSO_4 plus H_2.

KAGGWA (*interrupting him*): And what are you doing these days,
Kiwanuka?

KIWANUKA: I've just started teaching.

KARANJA (*laughing sarcastically*): Oh, a teacher!

KIWANUKA (*mildly*): Well, I enjoy teaching those village
children.

KARANJA: What? Ha, ha, ha! You mean you actually teach in a
village? How could you enjoy teaching in a *village*?

KIWANUKA: I like teaching in a village. I'm sure you lived in a
village before you joined a secondary school. And where would
you be if it hadn't been for teachers? You wouldn't have been
able to come to this un—

KARANJA: Yes, I did come from a village, but that's because my
parents were not progressive. Well, I'm not like that. I'm a
modern, civilized man. No more villages for me, thank you.
When I graduate in a few months time, I'll live in a big city
like Nairobi. And I won't waste my time teaching . . .

KAGGWA (*interrupting him*): Would you like to be taken round our campus, Kiwanuka?

KIWANUKA: I would love it. I've heard so much about this university but it's the first time I've visited it.

KAGGWA: Come, Karanja, and I will take you round.

They begin to leave. KARANJA *walks out first, but* KAGGWA *pulls* KIWANUKA *back.*

KAGGWA: 'I have professed me thy friend, and I confess me knit to thy deserving with cables of perdurable toughness: I could never better stead thee than now.' Er – could you lend me five shillings?

KIWANUKA *removes his wallet from his pocket as the curtain falls.*

CURTAIN

SCENE TWO

Scene: the same as before but eight months later. It is vacation time but KAGGWA *has stayed on in college. He is wearing the same outfit as before. He is writing at the table. He shifts about in his chair. Finally, he gets up, flinging the pencil down.*

KAGGWA: I give up – I just cannot write anything. (*Gets up.*) Oh, this vacation! There's nobody around: the College is so dull. There's nothing to do; life is bare; everything is so dead – it's driving me crazy!

A knock.

KAGGWA (*exasperated*): Oh, come in. (*Nobody enters.*) Well, come in if you want to, or stay out for good. Do either one or the other, but don't stand outside getting on my nerves.

KARANJA *walks in. He's wearing the same outfit as before except that he now has a black coat.*

KARANJA: Hello, hello, hello, Kaggwa!

KAGGWA: Why, hello Karanja! This is a pleasant surprise! (*They shake hands.*) I haven't seen you for ages. And what is the successful old graduate doing these days? You're looking very prosperous, old chap!

KARANJA (*thumbs in his coat lapels, modestly*): Well, I'm quite prosperous, you know. I have a wonderful job with the Shell Company. I am paid one-thousand-three-hundred shillings per month!

KAGGWA: Lucky chap! I've still got to slog. My finals are still a long way off!

KARANJA (*looking at the bookshelf and laughing*): Books, books, books! I'm glad that I've left all this behind me! Yes, sir, life is different for me! You won't find any books in my room. No, sir! I have a super new car, I have money to go to pictures any time I like. Guess what I do every day after work: booze, old man, booze! I drink myself under the table! I have so much cash that I can enjoy life to the full!

KAGGWA: Well . . .

KARANJA: And you'll never guess what: I'm engaged.

KAGGWA: Now why should you want to do a stupid thing like that? An intelligent man like you!

KARANJA: A wonderful girl, her education is far inferior to mine and so I'll be the boss in the house. No equality of the sexes for me! She admires me for being a graduate! (*He walks up to the table and picks up the exercise book. Reads aloud*) 'The Yellow Maize-Patch'. What's this?

KAGGWA: Oh, you know, 'All the world's a stage.' I'm writing a play for the drama competition.

KARANJA: Oh yes, of course. And you're churning out the usual play about the African village, and the chief being ill; about his son dramatically returning home from civilization in time to save his people, and all the rest of it . . .

KAGGWA: Well, yes. You know that these plays with a traditional air always go over well – although the audience usually laughs at the wrong moments.

> 'O brave new world,
> That has such people in't!

I wouldn't want to disappoint them. So I take a theme from a play by Ibsen or some other dramatist and Africanize it.

KARANJA: Don't forget to throw in the usual set, with bamboos, and to dress your actors in barkcloth. That usually impresses the adjudicators! It will get you the marks, you know. (*Turning away.*) But why should one waste one's time writing stupid old plays?

A knock is heard.

KAGGWA: Come in.

KIWANUKA *walks in. He is dressed casually.*

KIWANUKA: Hello, Kaggwa. Hello, Karanja. I just thought I would drop in to visit you. Besides (*hands* KAGGWA *a parcel*), your mother asked me to give you this parcel of food. She's worried about you because you haven't gone home for the vacation. She says that you don't even write to them . . .

KAGGWA (*taking the parcel*): Thank you.

KIWANUKA: Don't you think you should write to your family now and then?

KAGGWA: Yes, but look here, Kiwanuka, what can I write to them? They've got hardly any education while I will soon be a graduate. They wouldn't be able to understand me. They know nothing of the great writers. What have my parents in common with me?

KIWANUKA (*amazed*): What? You mean you can't even write to your parents just because they haven't read Shakespeare and Shaw? But Shakespeare should help you to understand people better and to sympathize with them, even if they are your intellectual inferiors! (*Shrugs.*) Is that —

KARANJA (*who has been trying all this time to place* KIWANUKA): Oh – now I've got it. You're the village schoolteacher. Ha, ha, ha!

KIWANUKA: Yes, and I like teaching in a village.

KARANJA: But don't you want to be progressive? Don't you want to teach in a city? To live in a nice big house with electric lights, to have a radiogram, and a Mercedes or a Chev.?

KIWANUKA: No, thank you. I love the village. I love teaching children while the world is still something new and mysterious and wonderful to them. There's nothing so satisfying as evoking a response from such children! But you can't understand, I have a radio but I don't want a car or radiogram. I love talking to people and being with them, even if they are simple. And although I'm not clever, I enjoy reading books.

KAGGWA (*quotes Keats*):

> 'Love in a hut, with water and a crust
> Is – Love, forgive us! – cinders, ashes, dust!'

Ugh! What were you saying?

KIWANUKA: I was asking you why you don't go home during the vacation. Why do you stay here?

KAGGWA: I must study for my finals. But the College is so, so bare these days, so dead: there's hardly any life here. I almost feel sick of it all . . .

KIWANUKA (*bewildered*): If you're tired of it, go home!

KAGGWA (*laughs bravely*): Tired of it? Oh no. I must study hard for my degree. I want to be like Karanja here – get a good job with a wonderful salary. Then others will say of me,

> 'He doth bestride the narrow world
> Like a colossus!'

KIWANUKA: By the way, did you hear of the death of Mulindwa? – the fellow who graduated from this University a few years ago.

KARANJA and KAGGWA *gasp, not really concerned about Mulindwa but each seeing himself in Mulindwa's place – for a moment only.*

KARANJA: Dead? Mulindwa's dead?

KAGGWA: I can't believe it! What did he die of?

KIWANUKA: Well, the doctors say that he died of cirrhosis of the liver induced by excessive drinking.

KAGGWA: I can't believe it – old Mulindwa dead! Why, just a couple of years ago, he was hale and hearty. He had a wonderful job with Stanvac; he was paid a fantastic salary, he had a lovely big car . . . And now he's dead: I just can't believe it.

KIWANUKA: Unfortunately, that is the way of life, and we must accept it. Some day I'll die; some day you'll die.

KARANJA (*hoarsely*): Don't say that! *Don't* say that!

KIWANUKA: Why, are you afraid of dying?

KAGGWA: Aren't you?

KIWANUKA: I'm not looking forward to death, but I'm not afraid of it. I've got enough out of life not to be afraid of death when it comes. (*To* KARANJA) But I don't see why you should be afraid of death. Your science tells you that matter can't be destroyed. You'll only undergo certain chemical changes, that's all.

KAGGWA: You're not afraid of death? You mean you believe in God!?

KIWANUKA: Perhaps I do, perhaps I don't . . . I don't know. But everything I do means a lot to me. Everything I have done has meant a lot to me and continues to mean a lot to me, no matter how long ago I did it. Everything means something while I am alive; and may continue to do so after I'm dead in the eyes of the world . . . But you won't understand. (*Change of tone.*) But what a lovely campus you've got here. It must be wonderful to sit on the green grass under a tree and read.

KAGGWA *and* KARANJA *regain their composure. They laugh.*

KARANJA: Don't be ridiculous! Sit under a *tree*? What is the library for? All the books one needs are in the library. And it has a wonderful atmosphere for studying. Only an idiot would think of studying in the open!

KIWANUKA (*to* KAGGWA): But at least *you* believe in reading in the open! Surely you must if you read Wordsworth!

KAGGWA: Why should one study in the open? Yes, I read Wordsworth, but that doesn't mean that I should study like a caveman instead of a modern civilized human being!

KIWANUKA *stares at* KAGGWA, *amazed. Then shrugs.*

KARANJA: I must say good-bye now, Kaggwa. Kiwanuka, would you like me to give you a lift in my Opel?

KIWANUKA: No, thank you. I have a bicycle.

KARANJA (*laughing in a superior way*): A bicycle! Well, good-bye, Kaggwa. Good-bye, Kiwanuka. It's been nice meeting you.

KAGGWA (*as he leads* KARANJA *out, says softly, so that* KIWA-NUKA *doesn't hear him*): I have professed me thy friend, I confess me knit to thy deserving with cables of perdurable toughness. I could never better stead thee than now! Could you lend me five shillings?

KARANJA: Sorry, old chap. I'm rather broke at the moment. I would help if I could. Good-bye. (*He leaves.*)

KIWANUKA (*looking at his wrist-watch*): I didn't realize it was so late! I'm afraid I must leave you too, Kaggwa. Any message for your parents?

KAGGWA: Thank them for the parcel and say that I'm fine.

KIWANUKA: All right. Good-bye, Kaggwa.

KAGGWA: Eh – could you lend me two shillings?

KIWANUKA: Why, of course. (*He takes out his wallet and gives* KAGGWA *five shillings.*)

KAGGWA: Thank you. Good-bye.

> KIWANUKA *leaves.* KAGGWA *walks back towards his seat; he puts the money into his pocket; sits down; scratches his head; and then jumps up, flinging the pencil aside.*

KAGGWA: Oh, damnation. I can't do any work. Why is the vacation so dull?

> 'Tomorrow and tomorrow and tomorrow
> Creeps in this petty pace from day to day!

Oh, why does college seem so terribly bare, so pointless? Why is life empty and dead? Oh, well, let's go and have some booze. (*He laughs, a little hysterically.*) There's always that.

CURTAIN

John Bing

THE WALL

A wall of simulated stone extends from a point ten feet from the front of the stage to within five feet of the back curtain. Two chairs face each other on opposite sides of the wall. During the play the music is modern and the lighting continually dims. During the performance from seven to ten people walk around on each side of the stage and cross in front of and behind the wall, carrying newspapers, brief-cases, lighting cigarettes, etc. When needed they enter into the world of the two main characters as directed in the script.

A: I've never seen this wall, although I think I've been here before. I can't see the end of it in either direction. I wonder whether it would fall apart if one or two of the bigger stones were dislodged. What does a wall like this hide?

B: This wall has been here ever since I can remember. Each year weeds grow thicker around the bottom stones and new spikes of grass dry in clusters of dirt between the rocks. What am I being protected from? Do I need protection? Even now, with darkness near, I have only to raise my voice and someone will come. Who is against me? People don't have the respect for others that they used to have, or the fear. No reason to take chances. (*He puts barbed wire on top of the wall.*) This should discourage anyone from trying to climb over.

A: What's going on? How did that barbed wire get there? Maybe the barbed wire is there to keep someone from escaping. If I could just see? (*He goes up and tries to look over.*) No, it's too high. All these people just walk by. None of them seem interested in this wall. I might be able to find out who's behind it. I know there are more ennobling battles than sweating over some stones, but men usually make an even poorer match for their abilities. (*He goes to take down a stone.*)

B: I knew the barbed wire was needed. Someone is trying to break through. He's taking out the stones. (*Calls to person walking by.*) Look! If he takes away any more that wall could crumble.

FIRST STRANGER: I'm sorry, sir, but I'm afraid I can't stop to talk.

B: Wait! Please! I've done nothing to harm him. Why does he want to tear down the wall?

FIRST STRANGER: If you don't mind I have an engagement in five minutes. Excuse me. (*Exits.*)

A: This is hot work. (*He goes towards the chair.*) Excuse me, sir. (*He sits down and mops his brow. He turns to* SECOND STRANGER.) Well, I've taken some of the stones down. I think I'm making progress. It won't be long now.

SECOND STRANGER: Well, very good, I wish you luck. (*Pause.*) Now, if you'll excuse me; I have a very important conference.

A: (*to* THIRD STRANGER): I think I'm doing a good job of breaking through.

THIRD STRANGER: I'm sure you are. (*Pause.*) Well I must be going.

B: Huh, he's stopped. I wonder if he ever intended to actually break through? I guess he was just curious. He would probably have been scared off if he had seen me. (*He gives coin to beggar moving by him.*) This wall is strong: he's hardly weakened it at all. I wonder if it was really meant to protect me. In a way it's too bad he gave up fooling with the wall. I'd like to have met him. You never can tell who might be a useful person to know. Oh well! (*He pauses.*) I wonder if he's really gone. It wouldn't hurt to look. (*B. begins to take barbed wire down; when he has finished he takes a few stones off.*)

A: Hey! Someone else is trying to break through the wall. I

thought I was going to have to do all the work myself. I'd better wait a bit now. He might not necessarily be friendly. This stick will be a good weapon, just in case.

B: He's still there, I saw him for an instant and he had a stick in his hand. I don't like this. He seems to just be resting. He may start tearing the wall down again. Why does he stay there? I can't make any sense out of it. (*He calls to someone.*) Sir!

FOURTH STRANGER: Excuse me, please.

B: Could you . . .

FOURTH STRANGER: . . . if you don't mind I'm in a great hurry. (*He leaves.*)

B: (*to* FOURTH STRANGER): I'm sorry. (*To* FIFTH): Sir!

FIFTH STRANGER: Yes?

B: I'm sorry to trouble you about this. It's a small matter, but, eh, I would like to ask your help with a problem I'm having.

FIFTH STRANGER: Well, if you can be brief.

B: It concerns this wall.

FIFTH STRANGER: I'm not quite sure I know what wall you mean.

B: The wall right there! There's a person behind it that, well, that may not be safe. I'm sure he's trying to break through.

FIFTH STRANGER: Friend, I rather doubt that there is any wall. I certainly don't see one. I'm afraid you're working yourself up over nothing. I've known people whose unconscious fears have created walls between themselves and others. It may be you fear to lose what you have because you feel guilt about the way you gained it. You may imagine people hate you because you hate yourself. If this is the case, you have only to accept your achievements, accept your faults along with your abilities. Then, I think, you'll find that the wall has never really been there at all, but was only a projection of your own anxieties. Now, if you'll excuse me, I must run. I have a class to teach. (*He leaves.*)

B: (*hitting at the wall; calling after retreating figure of* FIFTH STRAN-GER): But this wall is real! Look, it's solid. Someone is tearing it down. Come back! (*Figure exits.*) Why does someone have to break in on me?

A: He hasn't done anything for some time. I think he's stopped working. If he leaves now I'll never know whether he actually was dangerous. He might have been friendly. Maybe I'll just take off a couple more stones myself and see what happens. (*He works a bit.*)

ᴑɪxᴛʜ Sᴛʀᴀɴɢᴇʀ (*interrupting work of A*): Pardon me. I couldn't help but see all the work you've been doing. May I offer a suggestion? Leave the wall alone. There is rare beauty in a wall, casual strength and sudden weakness. I don't think you've begun to appreciate it. Come over here and look at it for the first time. You want to destroy, to tear down a wall, and you call it curiosity. You want to distort, to scatter stone and grass, and you call it mastery. You want to exploit, to prove your ability, your strength and courage, and you call it exploration. You are fascinated with the ritual of picking at the beach with your blue shovel, and you fail to see the ripple of sand at the edge of the beach fall into white moods of wave and far cloud. You live in many dimensions of space; half the horizon and the sky are free from the wall and they have barely been seen. Seek the beauty in these and learn to know reality and then try to appreciate the wall itself. See it as all clashes of light and shadow, and then you may understand it, and perhaps yourself as well.

A: You talk well, and I want to believe you. But you talk about a world that I can't wholly recognize. The deepest hurts and joys I feel are not a part of it. I'm not really sure why I work at this wall. It's not that I want to destroy: I want to build, but I don't know how to begin. I don't even know what I want to build but somehow I feel that it would not be with bricks and stones like these. So I continue to tear down. The reasons are deeper than pride and curiosity, I think, although these often give me strength. All my life I've searched in the desert, and the sand has fallen through my fingers. All my life I've searched in the ocean and the water has fallen through my fingers, and both are no more than sand and water. (*Pause.*) Perhaps I do know vaguely what I search for. A simple thing – a friend who will know me for what I am, selfish and vain, too arrogant

to be just a member of a group, too insensitive to be its leader –
half a poet and half a parrot. I blind myself with neat abstrac-
tions and a sense of form, and still am painfully aware that the
beautiful and ordered things standing useless are ugly. I make
friends by walking over friends so as to enjoy a sense of
mastery and the advantages friends can offer. I make friends
because I need continually to be assured people want me. And
it's all half life, ugly. I want a friend who will respect me: not
respect earned, not on my own merit, for I have none. I want a
friend who will know me for what I am and accept me for
what I am. It is this that drives me on past the brittle beauty
you point at. Even when I lose all sense of hope and direction,
this is behind my fumbling after mastery and accumulation.
Yet, I must seek for this other person, at any risk, for the sake
of confession, both hearing another and being heard in turn
for the sake of forgiveness. For this reason, at any risk, I must
tear down the wall. (*Goes to work.*)

SIXTH STRANGER: I'm sorry that we can't understand each
other. The world holds great beauty. (*He leaves and A continues
to work at the wall.*)

B: He's started again. I don't think he's going to stop. Now is the
time for me to leave. Projected fears or real enemy, I can still
walk away. (*Pause.*) Why do I kid myself? I stay by this wall
because there's no other place to go. (*Pause.*) He's taking off
another stone. He could be dangerous. (*He weighs a couple of
stones in his hand.*) I stay by the wall because he might not be an
enemy, and yet because I'm afraid he is. Is this a contradiction?
Is it a contradiction to want a friend and to know oneself too
well to expect friendship? This wall has been here all my life.
There have been other walls, much like this one, or has there
always been only this one? Have I ever crossed any of them?
I can't remember. I am lonely and afraid. Afraid of my loneliness, more than I am afraid of the movement behind the wall.
Yet afraid of that too. And all conspires to keep me here, by
the wall, waiting. I want to leave and yet am afraid to turn
away, both because I want to meet the outstretched hand
that is open, and because I am afraid to turn my back on the

outstretched hand that is closed. I must remain here while he tears down the wall – and I must help him tear it down. (*They both tear down the wall.*)

When they have finished, the music shifts to a formal motif, and both, as they catch sight of each other, pick up masks they find lying near them and hold them to their faces. All other actors leave the stage. It is almost dark now, but one can still distinguish form. A moderate spotlight lights the centre of the stage. They move formally into the spot, towards each other, bow stiffly, still with masks raised, and perform a formal dance around the stage while the spot stays on the centre. They finish back at the centre. The spot dims. They bow again and then walk back to chairs on each side of the stage and slump down, unmasked, facing away from each other, and the masks roll out of their hands on to the floor.

Contributors

Tunde Aiyegbusi is a Yoruba from Nigeria. He attended Ibadan Boys' High School and Government College, Ibadan, and is now an English Honours finalist in Makerere.

Tilak Banerjee was born in Calcutta in 1943 and in 1947 came to Uganda. He entered Makerere in 1960, and is now a third-year English Honours student.

John Bing studied at Yale. He came to Kampala with the Teachers for East Africa scheme and took his Teaching Diploma at Makerere in the following year, 1962.

Tom Chacha was born in Tanganyika and educated in Kenya at St Peter's, Nairobi, and Kabaa High School; he came to Makerere in 1960 and is now in his final year as an undergraduate in the Arts Faculty.

Valentine Eyakuze went to St Mary's, Tabora, and from 1951 to 1957 studied medicine at Makerere, where he won many prizes, including the B.M.A. Essay prize. He became M.R.C.P., Edinburgh, in 1963.

Joseph Gatuiria was born in Kenya and educated at Alliance High School. He gained his B.Sc.(Econ.) at Makerere in 1964. He now works as a development and planning economist in the Kenyan Ministry of Finance and Economic Planning. Kariuki appeared in *A Book of African Verse* in a slightly different form.

Gabriel Gicogo was at school in Nyeri and took an Honours Geography degree at Makerere in 1963. He is now in the R.G.A.'s office in Embu.

M. M. Haji was educated in Zanzibar. He came to Makerere in 1954 and in 1958 gained an Arts degree. He has worked for the Zanzibar Civil Service, at one time as Minister for Education and Information.

Anthony Hokororo came to Makerere in 1955 and gained his B.A. in 1959 and a Diploma in Education a year later. He is now at Carleton University, Ottawa, Canada.

Michael Kaggwa was educated at St Mary's College, Kisubi, and graduated from Makerere in English Honours 1960. Until recently he was with the Uganda High Commission in London, and has now returned to Uganda.

Solomon Kagwe was born in Nyeri in 1939. He was educated at Makerere College, where he gained his B.A. in English, History and Political Science in 1964. *To a Farm in the White Highlands* has been broadcast by the BBC and Radio Uganda.

Jonathan Kariara was born in the Nyeri District of Kenya in 1935. He was among the first English Hnoours students at Makerere (1955–60), and is now Senior Book Production Officer with the East African Literature Bureau in Nairobi.

M. Karienye is now a finalist in History Honours at Makerere. He has a regular column in the *Weekly News* under the name of Karienye Yohanna.

Cuthbert Khunga, a Malawian, was educated at Dedza Government Secondary School, and came to Makerere in 1960; in 1963 he gained his B.A. in English, History and Political Science. He was the first African to become a Regional Information Officer in Nyasaland and is now in the Foreign Service of Malawi in West Germany.

Violet Kokunda comes from Ankole in Uganda. She is now a second-year History Honours student at Makerere. She was educated at Bweranyangi and Kyebambe Schools, and then at Gayaze High School, and has taken part in schools broadcasting for Radio Uganda.

James McCarthy was at Makerere from 1959 to 1961 for postgraduate studies in Forestry. He then became a forestry officer in Tanganyika, and subsequently returned to the U.K.

Ben Mkapa came to Makerere in 1957, where he graduated in English Honours in 1962. He has been D.O. in Dodoma and then went to the U.S.A. in 1962 on a Carnegie Fellowship in Diplomacy. He is now Assistant Secretary to the Minister of External Affairs in Dar es Salaam.

Joe Mutiga was educated at Kagumo Secondary School and Makerere, where he was awarded his B.A. in 1964. Since then he has been working as an Administrative Officer in Kenya. His writings have been broadcast by the BBC African Service.

John Nagenda was born in 1938 at Gahini, Rwanda, where his father was a missionary. He came to Makerere, where he edited *Penpoint,* in 1957, and in 1962 graduated in English Honours. He has been a radio and magazine critic, but his chief interest is in writing short stories and poems. At present he is working for a publishing firm in Nairobi.

Peter Nazareth was educated at Senior Secondary School, Kololo, and took an English Honours degree at Makerere in 1962. He was an editor of *Penpoint,* has published several critical articles, and has had a play performed by the BBC African Service. He is now at Leeds University.

James Ngugi was born in Kenya in 1938, went to Alliance High School, and graduated from Makerere, where he edited *Penpoint,* in English Honours in 1964. While an undergraduate he wrote *Weep Not, Child,* which was enthusiastically received on publication in 1964, *The River Between,* to be published in 1965, and a play, *The Black Hermit,* which was performed by the Uganda National Theatre at Independence. He has also written for the *Sunday Nation,* and is now at Leeds University.

N. G. Ngulukulu was born in Tanganyika and educated there, at Pugu, and at Makerere, where he graduated in Honours English in 1964. He is now studying at King's College, Cambridge. He was an editor of *Penpoint.*

David Rubadiri is a Malawian. Born in 1930, he studied English at Makerere, and later at Cambridge University. He was detained during the state of emergency in Nyasaland in 1959. For a time he was Principal of Soche Hill College, Limbe, but is now Malawian Ambassador to the United States. He is well known as a poet. Earlier versions of these three poems have appeared in other anthologies.

Joseph Waiguru was born in Nyeri in 1939 and educated at Kangaru Secondary School. He came to Makerere in 1959 and graduated in English, Economics and Political Science in 1964. The writings in this volume have been broadcast by the BBC African Service and Radio Uganda.

Elvania Namukwaya Zirimu was born near Entebbe in 1938, and learnt no English till the age of ten. She attended Budo and from there came to Makerere, where she qualified as a teacher. She is now taking an English Honours degree at Leeds University. Her play has been performed by the Uganda National Theatre, and by the BBC and Radio Uganda.